BALDWIN'S GUIDE TO
INNS of MISSISSIPPI

BALDWIN'S GUIDE TO
INNS of MISSISSIPPI

JACK and WINNIE BALDWIN

PELICAN PUBLISHING COMPANY
Gretna 2000

*The word "Pelican" and the depiction of a pelican are trademarks
of Pelican Publishing Company, Inc., and are registered in the
U.S. Patent and Trademark Office.*

Library of Congress Cataloging-in-Publication Data

Baldwin, Jack (John Thomas)
   Baldwin's guide to inns of Mississippi / Jack and Winnie Baldwin.
     p. cm.
   ISBN 1-56554-663-6 (pbk. : alk. paper)
    1. Bed and breakfast accommodations—Mississippi—Guidebooks.
  2. Mississippi—Guidebooks. I. Baldwin, Winnie. II. Title.
TX907.3.M7 B35 2000
647.94762'03—dc21

                                                  99-086887

Information in this guidebook is based on authoritative data available
at the time of printing. Prices, amenities, and restrictions of businesses listed are subject to change without notice. Readers are asked
to take this into account when consulting this guide.

Map by Steve Graves

Printed in the United States of America

Published by Pelican Publishing Company, Inc.
1000 Burmaster Street, Gretna, Louisiana 70053

CONTENTS

INTRODUCTION

Mississippi is more than magnolias and moonlight, but the pair are still perhaps the most charming aspects of this most Southern of the states of the Deep South. In cities like Natchez and Vicksburg, you still hear those slow, smooth drawls that soothe like warm honey on a cold morning. And along the Gulf Coast, you can still find some of the best seafood in America.

The state has produced Elvis Presley and William Faulkner; it is in the heart of the Bible Belt, but its coast is lined with gambling boats. It has known serious racial problems, and it continues its efforts to redress this issue. As with any locale, it is the people and not the landscape that make the difference. As we have traveled from Biloxi to Tupelo and from Vicksburg to Laurel, we have found them to be friendly and outgoing, piling one hospitable act after another on strangers.

Their inns reflect this attitude. Whether it is an antebellum mansion in Natchez or a turn-of-the-century home in Jackson, each has greeted us warmly and fed us well. All are welcoming and comfortable.

As with our other inn guides, we do not use a rating system. We judge each place on its own merits, not against another or against some artificial standard that we have devised. Our only criterion is whether we would be willing to spend the night. If our answer is yes, then you will find it included here.

We do offer this caveat. Not everyone enjoys the inn or bed and breakfast experience. If you are uncomfortable with personal attention, an occasional shared bath (common in Europe, but rarer and rarer in the United States), or eating breakfast with strangers, perhaps you would prefer the large hotels complete with room service. But if you want the flavor of the land and its people, unhomogenized, try one of these accommodations.

In addition to a complete profile on each establishment, this guide includes many line drawings, information about the town or city in which the inn is located, some suggested things to do there, a mention of good restaurants where applicable, and recipes when the innkeeper has been generous enough to share them with us.

Rates range from moderate to expensive, and we have included those prevailing when we were there. Prices are always subject to change, however, and they seldom go down. You usually get about what you pay for, so do not expect Nieman-Marcus furnishings at Wal-Mart prices.

As usual, we have personally visited and inspected every property listed, and we have stayed overnight in many. We have checked bathrooms, kitchens, bedrooms, common rooms, and grounds, as well as access and parking. Since we performed inspections for the Louisiana Bed and Breakfast Association for two years, we are especially concerned about fire safety and food preparation, so we have looked for smoke alarms, peeped in refrigerators, and explored behind shower curtains.

We have attempted to be comprehensive, but if your favorite inn is missing, we are sorry. Some have been omitted because we failed in our efforts to contact the innkeepers. Our rule of thumb is that we try calling the establishments five times at different times and on different days. If we do not reach a live person, we move on. Our reasoning is that if we cannot reach someone, then the reader may also have a problem. We do leave messages on answering machines, but often our calls are not returned. We try to set up appointments. Failing this, we sometimes "cold call" a B&B, but we prefer not to.

If the inn scene sounds good to you, call one and make your reservation for a romantic weekend or a relaxing getaway from the daily stresses of the job. More and more business travelers are also finding these accommodations ideal for their needs. Women especially seem to enjoy the secure atmosphere. If you find an inn not to be as we have described it, or if you wish to second our opinion, we would like your comments. Just drop a note to Jack and Winnie Baldwin, P.O. Box 277, Bernice, LA 71222-0277. Above all, enjoy your stay.

BALDWIN'S GUIDE TO
INNS of MISSISSIPPI

Mississippi
Bed and Breakfast Locations

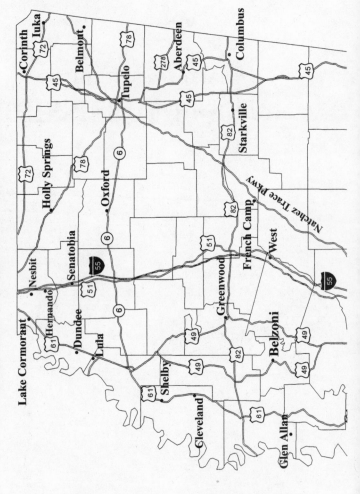

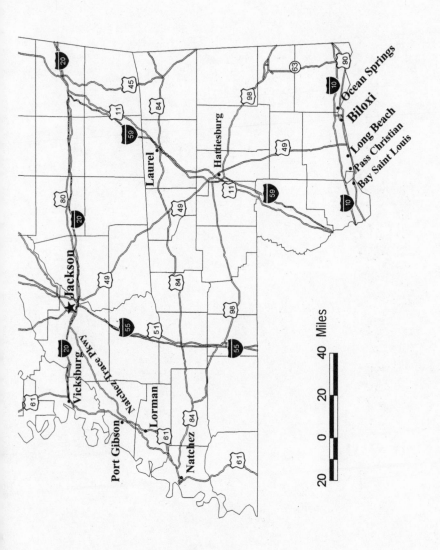

ABERDEEN

Founded in 1837 by Robert Gordon and named for Scottish Aberdeen, the town, with its location at the head of the Tombigbee River, was a major port by 1850. It was the seat of Monroe County and became prosperous before the Civil War, shipping cotton out and bringing finished goods in. It retained its position until the railroad replaced the river as a preferred mode of transport just after the turn of the century.

During Aberdeen's heyday, many imposing mansions were built in a variety of styles from Greek Revival to Art Deco, and the local visitors bureau has a brochure that gives architectural descriptions of 50 that have National Register status. Some are open to visitors during a three-day Aberdeen Pilgrimage every April. Others are open year round by appointment. It is also home to the Blue Bluff River Festival in October.

Properties include Prewett Place (1840), Lenoir Plantation (1847), Sunset Hill (1847), Gregg-Hamilton planter's cottage (1850), Holliday Haven (1850 Greek Revival), Shadowlawn (1874 Italianate-Victorian), Victoria (1879), and Lenoir Cottage (1890 Victorian), all open by appointment only. A classic Greek Revival mansion dating from 1850, The Magnolias, at 732 West Commerce Street, is open Monday-Friday from 9 to noon and 1 to 5. Admission is free.

The Evans Memorial Library at 105 North Long Street, founded in 1939 by Dr. William Augustus Evans, is known for its genealogical materials and is also home to a museum with exhibits that change regularly. It is open Monday-Thursday from 9 to 8, and admission is free.

Today, the town of nearly 7,000 people bases its economy primarily on chemical manufacture. For additional information, contact the Aberdeen Visitors Bureau, P.O. Box 288, Aberdeen, MS 39730, 1-800-634-3538, fax: 662-369-6489.

Huckleberry Inn

Huckleberry Inn
500 South Hickory Street
Aberdeen, MS 39730
1-800-565-7294 or 662-369-7294
Fax: 662-369-2478
E-mail: huckleberryinn@hotmail.com
Web site: www.bbonline.com/huckleberry/index.html

Eight rooms with private baths in 1908 two-story National Register house in Historic District of Aberdeen. Antique furnishings. TV, phone available, refrigerator upstairs. Full Southern gourmet breakfast. Other meals by request at $20 per couple. Well-behaved children only, no smoking, no pets. Reservation deposit required. Innkeeper Paula Thorpe. Rates $55-$95. Senior discount. AX, DS, MC, V. Pays commission to travel agents.

Dr. Joseph W. Eckford built Huckleberry in 1908 for his 30-year-old bride Gertrude Bumpus. Located in the heart of the Historic District, the inn is three blocks from downtown, about two miles from the Tombigbee River, and features an acre of informal gardens. Interior decorations include a mural in the dining room depicting a nearby cypress swamp.

Innkeeper Paula Thorpe, who only opened the inn in December 1998, also offers a variety of special packages including honeymoon, small party, rehearsal dinner, and special evening meal. Even though smoking is not allowed in the house, guests may do so on the porches or in the gardens.

The day we visited Huckleberry Inn, Paula had workers there replacing ceiling molding and making other decorative changes. She said since she had only been there a short time and wanted to add some personal touches, she planned to redecorate some of the guestrooms. She was also making major changes in the front and side garden areas, including a new picket fence across the front yard.

Paula said her breakfast includes French toast with blueberry sauce and whipped cream, hash browns or grits, hash-brown casserole, muffins or bagels, yogurt parfait, and coffee or tea, all served on antique crystal and china. She has furnished a recipe.

Poppy-Seed Bread

3 cups flour
2¼ cups sugar
1½ tbsp. poppy seeds
1½ tsp. baking powder
1½ tsp. salt
3 eggs
1½ cups milk
1 cup oil
1½ tsp. vanilla
1½ tsp. almond extract
1½ tsp. butter extract

Combine dry ingredients. Add eggs, milk, oil, and flavorings. Pour into two greased loaf pans. Bake at 350 degrees for 60-65 minutes. Cool completely in pans. Makes two loaves.

Sauce

¾ cup sugar
¼ cup orange juice
½ tsp. vanilla
½ tsp. almond extract
½ tsp. butter extract

Bring all to boil. Pour over warm bread in pans.

Morgan's Bluff
20136 Adams Road
Aberdeen, MS 39730
662-369-6521

Three rooms with private baths in 1989 country home. Contemporary furnishings. TV, phone available. Full Southern breakfast. Children welcome, no smoking, call about pets. Innkeeper Joe Morgan. Rates $45-$75. Senior discount. No credit cards.

Joe Morgan was just getting back into the swing of operating his bed and breakfast when we dropped by. We had called ahead, and he was waiting for us on the front porch. As we started inside, he told us that the B&B had been a project of his wife (Lynn) until her death 16 months before. He added that at first he was hesitant to try operating on his own, but that once he got started, things were working out well. He said that recently he had taken two women as the only guests, and that was okay, but that he probably would not feel comfortable accepting one woman if there were no other guests.

The two women had specified continental breakfast, but when he fixed full Southern—eggs, grits, sausage, biscuits—one morning, they cancelled their order for "just Danish and coffee." Actually, he will prepare just about anything his guests desire.

Overlooking a small lake, the two-story structure was built almost entirely by Joe, and everyone calls it "the house that Joe built." The lake contains bass, red-ear bream, and Mississippi catfish that weigh as much as 10 pounds. If you want to try your luck, he has fishing poles available. Joe said that the lake is an old one and badly silted, and that he is planning to build a larger dam behind the present one to enlarge and deepen the impoundment.

Out back he showed us a large wood-burning furnace that provides heat and hot water to the house. Built by a company in Tupelo, the heater requires filling once a day in winter and about every three weeks in summer. The house has total electric backup, but he seldom has to use it. Joe has had a full career, having worked for the FBI, Eastern and Northwest airlines, and as manager of the local golf club. Retired from these occupations, he finds that innkeeping keeps him busy.

When Joe and Lynn first built their house, they called it Morgan's Hilltop Inn. Joe says that they decided to change it to Morgan's Bluff because of a sheer bluff on the property. The steep drop-off was caused by the earthquake of 1811—the one that formed Reelfoot Lake in Kentucky and made the Mississippi River run backward. Wolf Creek flows past the foot of the bluff, and the innkeeper often takes guests there to look for arrowheads, shark's teeth, and fossils that wash down from the precipice into the water. Dandelion, Joe's black Persian cat, is his main helper around the place.

BAY ST. LOUIS

Bay St. Louis has been a getaway spot for New Orleans people since the 19th century. It remains a busy place but with a friendly small-town quality. There are more than 50 shops and restaurants in "Old Town." Here, visitors may shop for art, clothing, jewelry, dolls, crafts, pottery, antiques, and most anything else their hearts desire. Restaurants abound, and when we visited waterfront-situated Dock of the Bay for lunch, the gumbo, shrimp salad, bread pudding, and Barq's root beer were delicious.

This town is truly an art colony, and with more than 20 galleries, it has reason to take pride in its designation. But it remains unpretentious. According to the *Atlanta Journal-Constitution,* "Nobody . . . wears pantyhose or neckties." And *Southern Living* adds, "This town is fun!" Activities sponsored here include the Crab Festival in July and "A Place of Art" in October.

For more information, contact the Hancock County Tourism Development Bureau, 408A Highway 90, P.O. Box 3002, Bay St. Louis, MS 39521, 1-800-466-9048 or 228-463-9222. They are open Monday-Friday from 8 to 5.

Bay Town Inn

Bay Town Inn
208 North Beach Boulevard
Bay St. Louis, MS 39520
1-800-533-0407 or 228-466-5870
Fax: 228-466-5668
E-mail: info@baytowninn.com
Web site: www.baytowninn.com

Seven rooms with private baths in circa-1900 home overlooking St. Louis Bay. Period furnishings. TV, phone in common area. Full Southern breakfast. Children over 12 only, no smoking, no pets. Reservation required. Innkeeper Ann S. Tidwell. Rates $90-$105. AX, DS, MC, V.

One hundred years old in October 1999, Bay Town Inn was built by L. A. Montluzin for his family. He was the son of Lt. Louis de Montluzin, a cavalry officer in the army of Napoleon. The elder Montluzin was awarded a medal for service to the emperor during the Battle of Waterloo, and Napoleon himself pinned the badge on his lieutenant. On the final day of the battle, Montluzin was struck by a piece of shrapnel, but the medal deflected it, saving his life.

The son came to Louisiana from France in 1855 and established a boys' school in New Orleans. The younger Montluzin left the city in 1878 for health reasons and settled in Bay St. Louis, where he opened a pharmacy—the fifth in the state of Mississippi. His turn-of-the-century home was built on a previous foundation and has high ceilings, cypress doors, and a wide central hall.

Montluzin lived here with four sons and two daughters. One son, who was a physician, even used an upstairs room for his office at one time. The eldest son was an engineer and died of yellow fever during the construction of the Panama Canal. The other two followed their father to become pharmacists, and one of them, Rene, inherited the house and lived in it until he was 92 years old. The mother never learned to speak English, considering it "a barbaric language," but she swam every day in the bay in front of the house, winter and summer. Mrs. de Montluzin died less than a month áfter her husband, apparently of grief.

The scenic location of Bay Town Inn gives visitors an unobstructed front-porch view of the waterfront from one of the highest points on the beach. A gigantic registered live oak in the front yard is credited with protecting the house from major damage during Hurricane Camille. They still gather pecans from side-yard pecan trees, and there is a 50-year-old magnolia near the street.

Innkeeper Ann Tidwell was absorbed with a pharmaceutical group when we were there, but she took time from her busy schedule to show us her beautiful and comfortable rooms. A typical breakfast would include homemade biscuits, scrambled eggs, broiled tomatoes, cheese grits, fresh fruit, orange juice, and coffee or tea.

Heritage House Bed & Breakfast
116 Ulman Avenue
Bay St. Louis, MS 39520
1-888-702-2686 or 228-467-1649
Fax: 228-467-1649
Web site: www.goldinc.com/bsl/heritage

Three rooms with two baths in 1905 Historic District home. Antique furnishings. Cable TV, phone, fax. Refrigerator stocked with juice, water, and soft drinks. Off-street parking. Full Southern breakfast. Children 14 and up only, no smoking, no pets. Reservation deposit required. Seven-day cancellation policy for weekends, 24-hour for weekdays. Owners Winston and Alma Levy. Innkeeper Paul Larsen. Rates $95-$125. MC, V.

Heritage House, built about 1905 by E. F. Drake, a prominent civil engineer in Bay St. Louis, is still known locally as the Drake House. Present owners Winston and Alma Levy purchased the turn-of-the-century home and restored it in 1989. Today, it stands surrounded by azaleas and camellias that nestle under magnolias and live oaks.

The inn provides three spacious, comfortable, and tastefully decorated guestrooms and a sitting room/den located on the second floor. All three bedrooms have names—the French Room, the Victorian Room, and the Magnolia Room. The downstairs common rooms include a living room, dining room, and music room where guests may play an antique piano.

The inn is within walking distance of the beach, a health club, and several shops and restaurants. Paul Larsen, brother-in-law of the owners, manages the bed and breakfast and is the chef, with a seemingly unbounded culinary imagination. His full breakfasts include omelets, ham, steak, grits, broiled stuffed tomatoes, steamed asparagus spears, a fruit cup with a special Japanese sauce—and fresh biscuits always. Visitors have a choice of where to take breakfast—in the formal dining room or on the veranda.

BELMONT

Like many small turn-of-the-century Southern towns, Belmont is a railroad town. Even though there was a community here before the rails came through, it was the arrival of the trains that made the village. With the railroad came lumber operations, which actually centered on nearby Golden, where the sawmill was located. But Belmont was the trade center. Farmers in the surrounding countryside also came to Belmont for their supplies.

Eventually the timber was all cut, and farming declined, but Belmont managed to hang on. Today, the town has about 2,000 people, and several industries have located here providing ample employment. It is said that Belmont's population doubles during the day because so many flock here to work. Despite some empty storefronts, the town is thriving.

Its Tishomingo County location about five miles east of the Bay Springs lock and dam on the Tenn-Tom Waterway makes Belmont an ideal base for outdoor recreation. Two nearby parks, Shook and Blue Springs, offer a variety of opportunities for fishing, picnicking, and related activities.

The one-day Bear Creek Festival is held the Saturday following Labor Day each year and features one of the largest antique-automobile shows in the Southeast, with more than 200 vehicles on display. Arts and crafts are included in this celebration that began in 1976.

Belmont Hotel
121 Main Street
Belmont, MS 38827
662-454-7948

Eighteen rooms with private baths in two-story 1924 Georgian-style brick building recently restored. Antique furnishings, Oriental rugs, 14-foot ceilings, crystal chandeliers. TV, phone available. Continental breakfast. Children welcome, smoking restricted, no pets. Reservation required. Innkeepers Ron and Pat Deaton. Rates $38.15-$43.60. AX, MC, V.

The oldest continually operating hotel in Mississippi, the Belmont was originally built in 1924 to entice passengers from the passing trains. Innkeeper Ron Deaton says that the only time the hotel has closed its doors was for a few days after the financial crash of 1929 and for several months just before he bought it.

Belmont Hotel

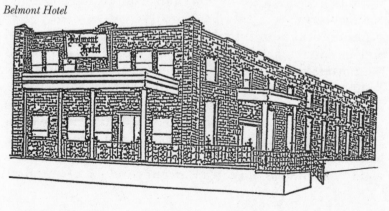

Ron and wife Pat took over in April 1996 from a lady who had run the place for 45 years. At first they rented out only three rooms downstairs while they renovated the second floor. Ron handprinted gold fleur-de-lis designs on the green wallpaper in the lobby and dining room and Pat used a sponge to create designs on the walls of the guestrooms.

Among their clientele are bikers who take a break from cycling the Natchez Trace just a few miles away, but Ron says he also gets many businesspeople, as well as family-reunion attendees. Guests are served a continental breakfast that includes muffins, bagels, English muffins, Danish, PopTarts, cereal, milk, juice, and coffee.

The railroad and its passenger trains are long gone, but the Belmont Hotel lives on.

BELZONI

Located in the heart of the Delta, Belzoni calls itself the "Catfish Capital of the World." It seems appropriately named, because as we approached the town we saw hundreds of catfish ponds interspersed among the cotton fields. A new museum and information center, known as the Catfish Capitol, gives visitors a look at all aspects of catfish farming. The center, designed by Oxford architect John Robbins, known for his work on the Statue of Liberty and the J. Paul Getty Museum, is housed in the old railroad depot. Mississippi-made handicrafts include ceramics, metalwork, and woodcarvings. Belzoni's World Catfish Festival is held in April featuring food, fun, and entertainment.

Another point of interest, the Ethel Wright Mohammed Stitchery Museum at 307 Central, and also known as "Mama's Dream World," is located in the former home of the artist. Tours are given by her daughter Carol Ivy, and visitors may see the family history drawn with the beautiful needlework that is Ethel's trademark. She is often called the "Grandma Moses of Stitchery," and some of her work is in the Smithsonian Institution. Admission is $2.

Just north of town, Wister Gardens developed by Frances

Chiles Henry and Wister Henry about 1937, contains 14 acres of azaleas, roses, daylilies, crepe myrtles, fruit trees, and other plants. Local fowl roam the acreage, including two varieties of swans and many ducks.

For more information, contact the Belzoni-Humphreys Development Foundation, 111 Magnolia Street, P.O. Box 145, Belzoni, MS 39038, 1-800-408-4838 or 662-247-4838.

The Cypress Inn
114 West Jackson Street
P.O. Box 254
Belzoni, MS 39038
662-247-1920

Seven bedrooms and three suites with private baths on first floor of circa-1900 Belzoni Hotel. Antique and reproduction furnishings. TV, phone available. Kitchen privileges. No breakfast. Children welcome, smoking restricted, no pets. Innkeeper Carol Ivy. Rates $35-$65. AX, DS, MC, V.

Located in downtown Belzoni, the Cypress Inn was once the Belzoni Hotel. At present only the downstairs has been restored. Innkeeper Carol Ivy's daughter, Amy, showed us through. Everything is furnished with antiques or reproductions beginning with the comfortable lobby. To the right is a room that they plan to make a real-estate office, and directly behind that is the coffee room, which will become a small gift shop.

Double doors lead from the lobby into the dining room, where Amy's grandmother and her friends play bridge weekly, and they had a rubber under way when we were there. The kitchen adjoins the dining room, and although the innkeeper does not serve breakfast, guests are allowed full use of both rooms to prepare their own meals. Gas range, refrigerator, and freezer are available.

The facilities, along with a small bar at the very back of the building—which Amy says is the first bar in Belzoni—are all available for receptions and parties, but the innkeeper does not cater. The guestrooms and suites are well appointed, with both singles and doubles available.

BILOXI

This resort city, protected by barrier islands from the pounding surf of the Gulf of Mexico, was the first place that we ever took our children on vacation—back in the late 1950s. It has been a favorite spot of ours ever since, although it has changed over the years, and with the advent of casino gambling at the ornate facilities that now dot the shore, Biloxi has become a booming new tourist destination.

The coastal drive along U.S. Highway 90 is still as scenic as ever, and the oak-shaded mansions across the highway from the water are still as grand as ever. Gaming has just added another dimension. One thing we do miss is Baricev's. A casino now occupies the spot once held by this fine old seafood restaurant. Otherwise, the town is just busier.

Originally located across the bay, Biloxi moved to its present site in 1719. In 1969, it was almost done in when Hurricane Camille blasted ashore with sustained winds of over 200 miles per hour, the strongest storm ever to hit the mainland of the United States. Two hundred fifty-six people died in this tragic horror in apartment buildings not capable of withstanding such a force. Most of the old mansions, though damaged, survived—and so did Biloxi.

Beauvoir, built in 1853 and the last home of Confederate president Jefferson Davis, has been restored along with the pavilions on either side. It was here that Davis worked on his autobiography, and many of the family furnishings are still in place. It is open daily, except Thanksgiving and Christmas, and admission is $6 for adults and $3.50 for children 6 to 15. Seniors and military get a 50-cent discount. Also located on the premises are the Presidential Library, just opened in 1998; Tomb of the Unknown Confederate Soldier; and a historic cemetery containing more than 700 Confederate graves.

Casinos include Beau Rivage, Boomtown, Casino Magic, Grand Casino, Isle of Capri, and the President at Broadwater Beach Resort. There are many festivals and events throughout the year—Mardi Gras on the Gulf Coast in February, the Oyster Festival in March, Confederate Memorial Day in April, Blessing of the Fleet in May, Mississippi Coast Coliseum Fair and Expo in

June, Biloxi Seafood Festival in September, and Victorian Christmas at Beauvoir in December to name a few. For a complete list and other information, contact the City of Biloxi Visitors Center, 710 Beach Boulevard, Biloxi, MS 39530, 1-800-245-6943 or 228-374-3105, fax: 228-435-6248, e-mail: visitor@biloxi.ms.us, Web site: www.biloxi.ms.us. They are open Monday-Friday from 8 to 5 and Saturday from 9 to 4.

Father Ryan House
1196 Beach Boulevard
Biloxi, MS 39530
1-800-295-1195 or 228-435-1189
Fax: 228-436-3063
E-mail: frryan@frryan.com
Web site: www.frryan.com

Fifteen units with private baths in 1841 two-story National Register home across highway from beach. Period furnishings. Cable TV phones with data ports, swimming pool, some whirlpools. Full breakfast. Afternoon tea. Children welcome, no smoking, no pets. Reservation deposit required. Seven-day cancellation policy for weekends with fee charged, 48-hour for weekdays. Innkeepers Rosanne McKenney and Carol Barker. Rates $100-$175, extra person $15. AX, DC, DS, MC, V. Travel-agent commission may be added.

Named for Fr. Abram Ryan, poet laureate of the Confederacy, and once his home, this bed and breakfast is one of the oldest houses on the Mississippi Gulf Coast. It was here that Ryan wrote much of his poetry, and it was here that he became a friend of Jefferson Davis. An unusual feature of the Greek Revival beach cottage is a large palm tree growing up through the middle of the front steps. Legend has it that when the good father moved in, he erected a cross at this spot to let people know that a priest was in residence. When he left the home, a storm blew away the cross and deposited a palm seed in its place. This is the tall palm that visitors see today.

Thomas Carter, a British architect, modified the house around 1900 and added the upper floor and a half. Its location directly across U.S. 90 from the Mississippi Gulf beaches makes it ideal for sitting on the balcony and watching the sea.

When we stayed at the house, innkeeper Carol Barker showed us into the Father Ryan room that looks out across the front gallery to the Gulf. Furnished with a tester bed complete with mosquito netting, it was spacious and airy. In addition to the bed, we had an Empire sofa, a small desk with captain's chair (handy for our laptop), an armoire with ample storage, bedside tables with lamps on both sides of the bed, and a table for coffeemaker and ice bucket. There is even a copy of a letter written by Father Ryan to a friend and headed "'Sea Rest,' Biloxi, Miss., January 13, 1882."

One of Ryan's poems, which was written on a shoebox and thrown on the floor after he heard of Lee's surrender, was preserved by his housekeeper. Visitors to Robert E. Lee's office at Washington and Lee University in Lexington, Virginia, will see a copy of it contained in Lee's coin purse. The first and last verses of the poem, entitled "The Conquered Banner," give one an insight into Ryan:

Furl that Banner, for 'tis weary;
Round its staff 'tis drooping dreary;
Furl it, fold it, it is best.
For there's not a man to wave it,
And there's not a sword to save it,
And there is not one left to lave it
In the blood which heroes gave it;
And its foes now scorn and brave it;
Furl it, hide it—let it rest.

Furl that Banner, softly, slowly,
Treat it gently it is holy
For it droops above the dead.
Touch it not
unfold it never,
Let it droop there, furled forever,
For its people's hopes are dead!

Guests have use of a full kitchen upstairs, but you should not use it for breakfast. Wait until 7:30 for one of Chef Gail Joachim's specialties, whether it be pancakes with praline sauce, a scrambled-egg-filled crepe, or a poached-egg dish. Father Ryan House and Gail have allowed us to use this recipe.

Eggs Oscar

4 artichoke hearts, quartered
$1/2$ cup chopped fennel bulb
1 cup sliced mushrooms
1 tbsp. chopped fresh herbs
Salt and pepper to taste
1 tbsp. oil or butter
2 large croissants, split and toasted
12 asparagus spears, steamed tender
4 thin slices Virginia ham, heated
4 eggs, poached
1 cup hollandaise with pinch saffron
1 cup white lump crabmeat
Fresh tarragon leaves for garnish

Sauté artichoke hearts, fennel, mushrooms, herbs, salt, and pepper in oil or butter. Place a croissant half on each of four plates. Arrange 3 asparagus spears on each plate. Top each croissant half with 1 slice ham. Divide artichoke and mushroom mixture among the four croissants. Place 1 egg on each veg-etable- and ham-topped croissant. Ladle saffron hollandaise over each egg. Sprinkle lump crabmeat over the top. Garnish with fresh tarragon. Serves four.

Green Oaks
580 Beach Boulevard
Biloxi, MS 39530
1-888-436-6257 or 228-436-6257
Fax: 228-436-6225
E-mail: greenoaks4@aol.com
Web site: www.gcww.com/greenoaks

Eight units in circa-1826 National Register home and cottage built on Spanish Land Grant. Antiques and family heirlooms. Cable TV, phone with data port, fax access. Golf packages, deep-sea fishing pack-ages, yacht charters, catering, cooking classes. Gourmet breakfast.

Green Oaks

Afternoon tea. Weddings, receptions, and other events. Children over 12 only, smoking outside, no pets. Reservation deposit with credit card required. 72-hour cancellation policy. Innkeepers Jennifer and Oliver Diaz. Rates $110-$175. All major credit cards. Pays commission to travel agents.

Jennifer Diaz had just had a wedding at Green Oaks, and when we pulled off busy Highway 90 into her drive, we found it blocked by rental trucks that had come to pick up the chairs and take down the white tent. She soon got that sorted out and graciously took us on a tour of one of the finest old mansions on the Gulf Coast.

Green Oaks is the oldest remaining beachfront house in Biloxi. The Greek Revival, raised-cottage-style home features a double-entry staircase from the ground up to the columned front gallery. Set among huge old live oaks and facing the sea, this proud mansion has ridden out numerous hurricanes that have destroyed many lesser structures.

Rooms are named for the family of Jennifer's husband, Judge Oliver Diaz, whose ancestor came to the area with Iberville in 1700 on the explorer's second voyage to the Gulf Coast. They include the Bosarge, Diaz, Carquot, Ladner, and Fountain rooms in the main house and Fayard, Ryan, and Moran rooms in the cottage. All are furnished with antiques, a couple have fireplaces and Gulf views, and another has a chandelier original to the house.

Lofty Oaks Inn

Lofty Oaks Inn
17288 Highway 67
Biloxi, MS 39532
1-800-280-4361 or 228-392-6722
Web site: www.bbhost.com/loftyoaksinn

Three rooms with private baths, plus cottage, in 1969 French-style farmhouse. Antique and other furnishings. TV, phone in all rooms but one, swimming pool, whirlpool. Full gourmet or Southern breakfast. Weddings, parties, and receptions. Children welcome, smoking okay, pets allowed. Reservation deposit with credit card required. Innkeeper Alice Jenkins. Rates $99-$125. MC, V. Pays commission to travel agents.

"This is the most romantic bed and breakfast on the Gulf Coast," Alice Jenkins says, "and the most fun." If you follow her through the house, you will tend to agree. Lofty Oaks is certainly different.

The place is filled with artifacts and memorabilia gathered on her trips around the globe. Her latest acquisition sits on the front porch—a bike-powered rickshaw. She says, "I will wow them when I ride this in the Mardi Gras parade."

Art, sculpture, and furniture from all over the world are incorporated into the décor of her inn. Alice is especially proud of what she calls her "thrift shop" art. It hangs everywhere and, according to her, the price was nearly nil.

In the main house, we were first shown the Oriental and Caribbean rooms. "I'm saving the best for last," she said, and then she took us to the Egyptian Room. The bed had a large gold Pharaonic head attached to the center of the footboard, about which she had an interesting story.

"I bought this thing in Cairo several years ago and brought it home. For a long time it hung on a tree in the yard, and then, one of my guests said, 'Alice, come up here, I want to show you something.' It was attached to the bed as you see it now." We had to agree that it was the perfect place for it.

Other unusual items included a matched pair of armchairs solidly inlaid with mother-of-pearl. An armoire, also inset with nacre, a Bedouin woman's handmade veil, several hookahs, an ornate chaise longue, a huge whirlpool, and many Egyptian items filled the room.

Throughout the house there are paintings, sculpture, artifacts, and memorabilia from such far-flung places as Indonesia, Africa, Europe, and most of the rest of the world. For example, when Alice took us out to the cottage, the first things we saw were two massive king and queen thrones of African origin. Whimsically, Alice had placed a huge plush gorilla in one of them. About this she said, "I started to hang him from the ceiling in the sitting room, but I was afraid it might frighten the guests."

Alice's breakfast may be full gourmet or Southern, whichever she is in the notion to cook. At any rate, she has graciously furnished the recipe below.

Egg-Puff Casserole

4-5 slices of fresh French bread, cubed
2 cups cubed ham or rendered sausage
3 cups grated cheddar and mozzarella cheese
3 tbsp. flour
1 tbsp. dry mustard
¼ cup melted butter
7 eggs, beaten
3 cups milk
Salt and pepper to taste (or your favorite spices)

Butter a 9" x 13" pan. Put the cubed bread on the bottom, and sprinkle ham or sausage on top. Put cheese on top of that. Mix flour, mustard, and butter in blender to make paste. Mix eggs, milk, and seasonings and slowly add to other mixture. Pour over other ingredients in pan. Cover and refrigerate overnight. Bake at 350 degrees for an hour or until puffed and golden.

Parker's Landing
7577 East Oaklawn Road
Biloxi, MS 39565
228-392-7717

Four units with baths on grounds of 100-hookup RV park. Eclectic furnishings. TV, phone. Full kitchen. No breakfast. Children welcome, no smoking, call about pets. Reservation deposit required. Innkeepers Dennis and Elva O'Brien. Rates $65-$110, weekly and monthly rates also available. AX, MC, V. Pays commission to travel agents.

Nestled near the banks of Parker Creek toward the back of Dennis and Elva O'Brien's RV Park, there are a cabin, lodge, and two efficiencies. The cabin is exactly that—one large room with bath and kitchen, and it is set slightly apart from the other buildings.

The structure that the O'Briens call the lodge was on the property when they bought it in 1996, and Elva thinks that it dates from the 1930s. It has three bedrooms, a living room, dining area, full kitchen, and one bath, making it primarily suitable for larger families.

Located upstairs over a large hall used for various park functions, the efficiencies each have a bedroom, bath, and kitchen. Elva says that a lot of their business in the guesthouses comes from people who have sold their RVs but who like to remain in touch with their still-traveling friends. Many of them are "snowbirds," she adds. She also notes that there is a boat ramp, but you must bring your own boat if you want to try your hand at fishing.

There is no breakfast here, but the kitchens make it possible for guests to prepare their own and other meals as well.

CLEVELAND

After being called Fontaine, Coleman (or Coleman's Station), and Sims, the railroad town of Cleveland, Mississippi, was finally incorporated in 1886. There are two stories about why it was named for the U.S. president. One was because he was the first Democrat in the White House since 1861 and the other because he rode the first train through from Memphis to New Orleans. Either way, Cleveland it is, and the railroad runs right down the middle of "Cotton Row," the shop-filled main street of this North Mississippi seat of Bolivar County. After a 1900 fire destroyed many of the downtown businesses, they immediately rebuilt using brick construction, and today the town maintains a lively, commercial atmosphere.

Cleveland is the home of Delta State University with over 4,000 students and a new performing arts center, which opened in 1995 with a 1,200-seat auditorium, offering upscale cultural events. The town is also in the center of blues country. According to his autobiography, W. C. Handy says that he learned about the blues while playing at a dance at the Cleveland Court House in 1905, and it was then that he became a blues man himself.

Numerous restaurants can be found here, but Cleveland is known for K. C.'s, a four-star establishment that features New American as well as Chinese food, and it also has an extensive wine cellar. Many festivals and events take place annually; the most popular is the Octoberfest, when more than 15,000 people crowd the town center the second Friday and Saturday of October.

For more information, contact the Cleveland/Bolivar County Chamber of Commerce, 600 Third Street, P.O. Box 490, Cleveland, MS 38732, 1-800-295-7473 or 662-843-2712. They are open Monday-Friday from 8 to 5.

Molly's Bed & Breakfast
214 South Bolivar Avenue
Cleveland, MS 38732
662-843-9913

Three rooms with private baths in two-story early-1900s former boardinghouse. Antique and hand-sculptured furnishings. TV, phone available. Full Southern breakfast. No children, no smoking, pets may be boarded with a nearby veterinarian. Innkeeper Molly Shaman. Rates $55-$65, extra person $5. MC, V.

Molly's Bed & Breakfast

Innkeeper Molly Shaman says her home was built during the early part of the 20th century and bought by a Ray family in 1912. It was eventually turned into a boardinghouse by Miss Mitty Ray and later into apartments. When Molly and her husband, Floyd, acquired the house in 1977, it was showing major signs of neglect, and they restored it as their family home. When their children all moved on, they decided to make it into a comfortable bed and breakfast, which it remains today.

We had the "Victorian Room," with two wingback chairs (more inns should consider this), a useful small secretary, and a massive Victorian dresser and bed, the latter with reading lights installed in the headboard (a major plus for us). The headboard was attached to the wall, so it did not rock every time we moved, and there was a rocking chair, six-panel 1920s wall mirror and, many of Molly's personal decorative touches.

The house is filled with art and sculptures by Floyd, who formerly taught art at Delta State University. Much of his work is wood and includes life-size statues of their sons as teenagers. Floyd made some of the furniture also. In the dining room there is a sideboard that he designed, and standing beside it is the whimsical "sidebird," a large ostrich that could be utilized as a stand.

One bedroom is named the "Watermelon Room," and once you enter it, you see why. Everything has a watermelon motif, including the Floyd-designed watermelon bed. The "Western Room" has wall paintings of Buffalo Bill and Gene Autry as well as a rolltop desk that belonged to Floyd's uncle. Floyd also designed the stained-glass "Flaming Watermelon" transom over their front door.

Molly brought a pot of early coffee to our room, and when we went down to breakfast, she served us delicious French toast, bacon, fresh fruit, and more coffee on their screened back porch, directly across from Floyd's studio. As we were leaving and told him that we were going to Oxford, he said some of his sculpture was on display at a gallery there.

COLUMBUS

Thomas Thomas built a trading post in 1817 on the site of what is now Columbus, and it was not long—certain things being necessary—before Spirus Roach put up a tavern. The Indians thereabouts called the community Possumtown, presumably because of Roach's appearance, but by 1821 it had been named Columbus. During the Civil War, there was an arsenal here, and for a time it was the state capital. It never came under Yankee attack, though, and as a result, over 100 antebellum homes have survived.

Memorial Day began in Columbus. Both Union and Confederate soldiers killed at the bloody 1862 Battle of Shiloh are buried in Friendship Cemetery, and when Confederate widows saw that Union graves were not being kept up, they rectified the problem themselves, starting what became a national holiday.

Some of the old homes are open on a daily basis, and more may be toured during a pilgrimage, complete with hostesses in period dress, the first week in April. Columbus is also home to Mississippi University for Women, which was founded in 1884. Tennessee Williams spent his first four years in the house that is now the welcome center.

If you want to see a Main Street program that has worked, you should go to Columbus. Downtown is definitely revitalized here. Not only have the storefronts, which actually contain viable businesses, been painted and/or restored, but the spaces on the floors above have been, in many cases, converted to apartments. Small town America still exists in Columbus, Mississippi.

For additional information, contact the Columbus

Convention and Visitors Bureau, 318 Seventh Street North, P.O. Box 789, Columbus, MS 39701, 1-800-327-2686 or 662-329-1191, www.friendship.columbus.ms.us. Or visit the Mississippi Welcome Center, Tennessee Williams Home, 300 Main Street, Columbus, MS 39701, 662-328-0222. They are open daily from 8:30 to 5:30.

Amzi Love Bed and Breakfast
305 Seventh Street South
Columbus, MS 39701
662-328-5413

Five bedrooms with private baths in 1848 National Register Italian-style cottage located in Historic District. Original antique furnishings. TV, phone. English garden. Full Southern breakfast. Dinner may be ordered at $50 a person. Receptions, teas, and bridge parties. Call about children, no smoking, no pets. Reservation deposit required. Innkeeper Sid Caradine. Rates $100-$125. Senior and extended-stay discounts. AX, MC, V.

This bed and breakfast is actually composed of two adjacent properties, the house that Amzi Love built for his bride, Edith Wallace, in 1848 and the earlier 1833 Lincoln House. The Love house is an Italianate Greek Revival home with Gothic arches. Many furnishings are original family pieces, not unusual when you consider that the home has always been occupied by descendants of Amzi Love. Owner Sid Caradine says that he is the seventh generation to live in the cottage and the first male in 100 years.

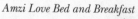

Amzi Love Bed and Breakfast

As he gave us a tour, Sid pointed out family heirlooms and identified the portraits of relatives. One such was an aunt holding a fan, and moments later Sid showed us the same fan displayed with other family pieces. In an earlier brochure Sid's mother, Betsy, sums up the house and its history quite well when she says, "Built along the lines of a cozy cottage Southern home in pre-war days, the furniture and fixtures bespeak not so much of grandeur but of comfort and good living."

Lincoln House came into the picture when Sid's wife, Brenda, left Memphis to marry him. She sold her Tennessee home, and they bought the house adjacent to the Amzi Love home. We stayed in the carriage house of the Lincoln building where we had the use of practically the entire ground floor. Our bedroom was spacious enough—with sufficient furniture plus a fireplace—to be called a suite. Just outside, a large common area provided more sitting room and a small semikitchen with microwave, sink, refrigerator, and coffee and tea makers. Sid had stocked the kitchen well with coffee and regular and herbal teas. The fridge contained a variety of soft drinks.

We had breakfast in the Amzi Love house, where Chef Sid served a Southern feast that included omelets, grits, biscuits, sausage, juice, and coffee. He will also do dinner if asked ahead of time. For $50 a person, expect such entrees as beef tenderloin and orange roughy.

Backstrom's Country Bed and Breakfast
4567 Highway 182 East
P.O. Box 2311
Columbus, MS 39704
662-328-7213

Three rooms with baths in 1980 country home. Antique furnishings. TV/VCR, phone available. Full country breakfast. No children, no smoking, no pets. Innkeeper Betty Joe Backstrom. Rates $75. MC, V.

Located on the edge of town, Backstrom's was a pleasant surprise. Outside, it appeared to be a handsome contemporary brick home; it was built in 1980. But that is only the tip of the iceberg. Practically all of the lumber, used in the doors, floors, wall paneling, stairs, railings, and even molding made by host Bill Backstrom, came from an old Tennessee country

*Backstrom's Country
Bed and Breakfast*

store run by Betty Joe's father. Some of the furniture, notably an elegant dining table, came directly out of the late-19th-century mercantile establishment.

Living-room walls are paneled two stories high with single-run boards—no cuts or joints mar the symmetry anywhere. The decor is largely family oriented, and every item in the house seems to have an interesting story attached to it. From the quilt on the living-room wall made by Betty's mother, to the stained-glass window on the second-floor living-room balcony constructed by Bill and incorporating the bottom of an amber-colored Coca-Cola bottle found under the store, to the wooden bench in the hallway made by one of their three sons, there is a uniqueness that surprises and attracts the visitor.

Bill's artistic talents are demonstrated over and over throughout the house. He did the sculpture, carved the wood, painted the portraits, blew the glass bottles, and constructed the cabinets. Betty insists, however, that her only talent is collecting.

All of the three upstairs guestrooms are attractive, but it was the Green Room that caught our attention. Bed, two dressers, stool, chair, table, and chest made up a seven-piece set of such delicate elegance that it is difficult to describe. Made in Grand Rapids in the early 20th century in a style that is vaguely art deco, each piece features a hand-painted floral design to complement its light-green original finish.

Breakfast with the Backstroms is full country, which means eggs, grits, sausage, biscuits, homemade jellies, fruit, juice, and coffee.

Cartney-Hunt House

Cartney-Hunt House
408 Seventh Street South
Columbus, MS 39701
662-329-3856

Two rooms with private baths in circa 1828 two-story Federal-style brick home. Period furnishings. Cable TV, phone. Continental breakfast. Children welcome, no smoking, call about pets. Reservation deposit required. Innkeeper Vicki Hardy. Rates $85. AX, MC, V.

The Cartney-Hunt House was not only the first brick home built in Columbus and one of few Federal-style houses in the South, it is also the first bed and breakfast to begin operations in this classic Mississippi town. James M. Cartney purchased a tract of land on what is now Seventh Street in Columbus in 1824 and by 1828 had erected the ell-shaped two-story building. Originally it was two rooms deep but only one room wide.

Cartney sold the home to Henry W. Hunt in early 1836. As the oldest brick home extant in Columbus, it is a striking example of a house type first introduced into America by Swedes settling in the Delaware River valley. The style was adopted by the Pennsylvania Dutch and Quakers and was once quite common along the Atlantic coast. However, it is rare in the Deep South.

Innkeeper Vicki Hardy notes that Seven Springs, a mid-18th-century home in King William County, Virginia, has a floor plan that is practically identical. She and husband Kirk bought their house from Columbus attorney Hunter M. Gholson. Gholson acquired the property in 1982, started restoration the next year, and won the Columbus Restoration Award for his efforts.

Despite having to care for her sick children the day we visited Columbus, Vicki graciously showed us through the entire original house, including the comfortably furnished upstairs guestrooms. Her continental breakfast includes home-baked breads and muffins, fruit, juice, and coffee or tea.

Fourth Avenue Cottage
912 Fourth Avenue South
and
Ninth Street Suite
403 Ninth Street South
Columbus, MS 39701
662-328-9575

Two units with private baths in, and on the grounds of, 1840 historic home. Antique furnishings. TV/VCR, phone. Full kitchen. Continental breakfast. Call about children, no smoking, no pets. Innkeeper Fran Brown. Rates $85. Extended-stay discount. MC, V.

Fourth Avenue Cottage

Ninth Street Suite

The 1840 Max Andrews House provides the setting for Fran Brown's Ninth Street Suite, and the Fourth Avenue Cottage is on the grounds. When guests book the suite, the innkeeper locks it off from the remainder of the house, giving them complete privacy, including a private entrance. Originally Miss Matilda Phillips' school, the building was later Green T. Hills' stagecoach stop. In those days it was known for good fried chicken and clean beds. The latter was something of a rarity, Fran says.

Visitors enter the front door into a foyer with the bedroom on the right and the parlor on the left. The bedroom contains an Empire sofa and queen-size four-poster bed, and the parlor has an 1850s chandelier that has been converted from gas to electricity. The self-catered continental breakfast includes home-baked breads, cereal, fruit, juice, and coffee or tea.

Fourth Avenue Cottage, where Fran's mother once ran a kindergarten, comes complete with kitchen, bedroom, and sitting area—just right for the businessperson on an extended stay. Like the suite, the cottage is filled with antiques, not so unusual since Fran is a dealer who also teaches at the Mississippi University for Women Demonstration School.

Liberty Hall
1521 Armstrong Road
P.O. Box 309
Columbus, MS 39703
662-328-4110

From Main Street turn south on Lemberg Road, go 1.25 miles, then go east on Armstrong Road for 1 mile. Three rooms with private baths in circa-1832 National Register property. Antique furnishings. TV,

Liberty Hall

phone available, swimming pool. Hiking and fishing. Full Southern breakfast or, if you prefer, continental served in room. Dinner by reservation. Children over 12 only, no smoking, no pets. Reservation deposit required. Innkeeper Sarah Fowler. Rates $85-$150. No credit cards.

Liberty Hall, built in 1832, remains in the family of the original builder. Descendants have lived here for five generations. The Fowlers came to Columbus from South Carolina seeking new and more fertile farmland. Many of the furnishings are original to the house, and everything is antique. The two-story quadruple-columned Greek Revival structure is filled with family portraits and other paintings and also features French country scenes on the upper panels of the dining room. These were done by a South Carolina artist who came here and lived on the premises, but the outbreak of the Civil War forced him to leave, and some of the panels are unfinished.

The day we got to Liberty Hall, housekeeper Dorothy Swanigan was the only one there, and the gate to the driveway leading up to the house was closed. We called on the car phone, and she said that she would open the remote-controlled gate for us. After several attempts, she finally managed to swing it open, and we proceeded up to the house, which stands on 600 acres just east of Columbus. Dorothy showed us through this impressive antebellum home with its period decor, and when we left, we called back to the house on the car phone to tell her that we had cleared the gate, and as we watched, it slowly swung to behind us.

White Arches
122 Seventh Street South
Columbus, MS 39703
662-328-4568

Five rooms with private baths in 1857 combination of Victorian Gothic, Greek Revival, and Italianate, two-story white home with cupola and three arches flanked by heavy columns. Original antique furnishings. TV, phone. Full Southern breakfast. Children welcome, smoking on balcony, no pets. Reservation deposit or credit card required. Innkeepers Sarah and Ned Hardin. Rates $100. MC, V.

The 1857 home of Sarah and Ned Hardin has a front turret, rising above the first and second floors, which tops a portico with four arched columns, the wider center area being the entryway. Slender columns complemented by fretwork railing support galleries on either side, and dark-green shutters adorn the windows. A Mr. Harris built the house, and the Hardins bought it from his descendants in 1968.

When genial Ned Hardin let us into the main hallway, what we saw was pure elegance. Original antique furnishings, about 70 pieces in all, filled hall, parlor, dining room, and library, where there were 150-year-old books, which also came with the house. Upstairs, the guest units were no different. Everything was antique.

Ned even showed us how he had gained space for the private baths by utilizing a hallway. But he carefully noted that it had been done in such a way that the home could easily be restored to the original condition.

The full Southern breakfast usually consists of eggs, bacon or sausage, grits, fruit, biscuits, jelly or jam, butter, orange juice, and coffee or tea.

CORINTH

Filled with historic buildings, this town of about 12,000 people was also the site of one the fiercest battles of the Civil War, the 1862 Battle of Corinth. Gen. P. G. T. Beauregard confronted the Union Army, but in hand-to-hand fighting his troops were driven out as they attempted to retake the town. Today, the visitor may see a reconstruction of Battery Robinette, a Union inner defense position, where the bloodiest fighting took place.

The grounds of the 1857 Curlee House contain the Civil War Interpretive Center, where visitors can watch a video about the battle. Curlee House is one of 16 Corinth homes on the National Register, and it is also a Mississippi Landmark. Sixteen-foot ceilings, period furnishings, and ornate plasterwork are featured in this antebellum mansion, which was one of the homes that served as headquarters for Union and Confederate generals.

Just outside town, the 1854 Federal-style Jacinto Courthouse is all that remains of what was once the political and cultural center of northeast Mississippi. Jacinto was the seat of Tishomingo County until 1870, when Tishomingo was divided into three counties—Alcorn, Prentiss, and Tishomingo. When the town declined, the courthouse became a school until 1908 and a Methodist church until 1960. The National Register property has been restored as a park area featuring walking trails with a replication of a doctor's office in an 1850 Victorian structure nearby. The Jacinto Foundation, Inc., operates the facility, and every year on July 4, the Jacinto Festival takes place at the courthouse with arts, crafts, concessions, entertainment, and old-fashioned political speeches.

Three golf courses, Pickwick Landing State Park, J. P. Coleman State Park, Tishomingo, and Bay Springs Lake, all within a short distance of Corinth, offer excellent opportunities for outdoor recreation including swimming, fishing, picnicking, and hiking.

For more information on Corinth activities, contact Tourist Information, The Alliance, 810 Tate Street, P.O. Box 1089, Corinth, MS 38835, 1-800-748-9048 or 662-287-5269, www.corinth.net. They are open Monday-Friday from 8 to 5.

The Generals' Quarters and Madison Inn Illustration by Scott Stephenson

The Generals' Quarters and Madison Inn
924 Fillmore Street
Corinth, MS 38834
662-286-3325
Fax: 662-287-8188
E-mail: genqtrs@tsixroads.com
Web site: www.tsixroads.com/~genqtrs

Five rooms with private baths in circa-1872 Victorian home. Period furnishings. TV, phone. Lounge on second floor. Full Southern breakfast. No children, no smoking, no pets. Reservation deposit required. 72-hour cancellation policy. Innkeepers Charlotte and Luke Doehner. Rates $75-$100. DS, MC, V.

A portrait of Robert E. Lee was hanging in the lobby, but it was Nathan Bedford Forrest, gloved right hand grasping his sword hilt, who looked down on us from the wall as we lay in the massive four-poster canopied antique bed in our suite at the Generals' Quarters. This bed and breakfast was so named by our innkeepers because most of the Union and Confederate generals found their way to Corinth at one time or another.

The bedroom was tastefully decorated and luxurious. Dresser and armoire matched the bed, which was flanked by a pair of wingback chairs and two bedside tables with lamps. A small writing desk and chair stood in one corner. The other, smaller room, with four banked, lace-draped windows across the back wall, was bright and airy with a table, two chairs, a very comfortable upholstered rocker, and a reading lamp.

This was our fourth night on the road, and we were happy to

have landed in such a spot. When we were talking to our host, Luke Doehner, earlier, we noted that he did not talk like a Mississippi boy, and he admitted that he came from the Washington, D.C.-Baltimore area. We had the innkeepers listed as Charlotte Brandt and Luke Doehner, but Luke told us that the partnership was now Charlotte and Luke Doehner, the couple having decided to be partners in more ways than one. Charlotte has many stories about their home and its history, since it has served as everything from an Episcopal church to a brothel.

Breakfast here might be, and for us was, Dijon Scrambled Eggs, fried ham, buttermilk biscuits, juice, and coffee or tea. The Doehners also cater dinners, receptions, weddings, and other functions.

Ravenswood
1002 Douglas Street
Corinth, MS 38834-4227
662-665-0044

Two bedrooms and one suite with private baths in two-story 1929 home on edge of Historic District. Antique furnishings. TV, phone. Hot-tub room, salon. Continental Plus breakfast. Well-behaved children welcome, smoking on three porches, small pets only. Innkeeper Ron Smith. Rates $75-$120. Senior discount. MC, V.

Arts and Crafts style Ravenswood, built in 1929 by local lumberyard owner and contractor Rufus Gaylean, features two original stained-glass windows in the Frank Lloyd Wright style. As

Ravenswood
Illustration by Ron Smith

is typical of this architectural genre, there are many built-ins, including living-room bookcases that flank a gas fireplace. Closets are cedar lined, and a total of 12 different varieties of wood are incorporated into the building. The ceiling moldings are hardwood, and the library, originally a child's room, has unique hand-cut baseboards and doorframes.

The downstairs guestroom has a hall bath, and upstairs is the two-room Gaylean Suite, with large private bath, and Flower Room. A common room on the second floor gives guests a spot to read or have morning coffee.

Ravenswood's backyard has a crescent-shaped Civil War breastwork built during the Battle of Corinth. According to innkeeper Ron Smith, it is one of very few such structures preserved on private property in Corinth. He also says that he has a ghost. A soldier was killed in the earthworks and still roams upstairs at night.

FRENCH CAMP

When Louis LeFleur built his inn at the French Camp site on the Natchez Trace in 1812, Choctaws and Chickasaws had already been there for decades. LeFleur married a Choctaw, and their son, after changing his name to Greenwood Leflore, went on to become a Choctaw chief and a state senator. Among the oldest surviving houses here are the 1840 Huffman Log Cabin dogtrot and 1846 Col. James Drane House. The cabin now houses the visitor center for French Camp Academy, and the restored Federal-style Drane house, also on academy property, may be toured free of charge. Today, French Camp is French Camp Academy, and vice versa.

This nondenominational Christian school was established by Scotch-Irish Presbyterians in 1885. Originally it was the Central Mississippi Institute for Girls and the French Camp Academy for Boys. When a fire destroyed the girls' school in 1915, the two were combined into French Camp Academy.

Supported by a variety of private funds, the academy currently has about 175 boarding students and 85 day students of all Christian denominations. Many of the predominately teen students are "at risk" because of broken homes or other problems, but not all. Even though the school asks for tuition, no one is turned away for lack of money.

French Camp Bed and Breakfast Inn
One Bluebird Lane
P.O. Box 120
French Camp, MS 39745
662-547-6835
Fax: 662-547-6790

Five rooms with private baths in main house and log cottage. Antique furnishings. TV, phone in common room. Full Southern breakfast. Children welcome, no smoking, call about pets. One-half reservation deposit required. Innkeepers Ed and Sallie Williford. Rates $50-$60. No credit cards. Pays commission to travel agents.

The main house of French Camp Bed and Breakfast is actually two, two-story log houses joined with a modern central addition. One log portion contains the guest accommodations, along with a nearby two-bedroom log cabin. We chose the downstairs suite with a comfortably large sitting room and twin-bedded sleeping quarters. The bedroom was smaller but adequate and well furnished with chest of drawers and dresser.

Other bedrooms are upstairs, and one has a double bed and the other twins. The cabin, with its two upstairs bedrooms, is only rented as a unit and has a full kitchen and a freestanding woodburning fireplace in the living area.

French Camp Bed and Breakfast Inn
Illustration by Sallie Williford

Innkeeper Sallie Williford greeted us with coffee and cake and sat to chat as she sipped her hot tea. She explained that the B&B is owned by French Camp Academy, and she and her husband, Ed, had managed it for the last several years. Students from the academy help her with B&B chores after school, and three of them came in while we were there.

GLEN ALLAN

Glen Allan is small, but its location on the shore of Lake Washington makes it attractive to visitors, especially those interested in outdoor activities. The main sights seem to be a branch library and an unusual Methodist church. The white frame house of worship is not typical church architecture—no steeple, no columns across a front gallery—but an attractive building nonetheless. It caught our eyes at once, but until we got close enough to read the sign, we had no idea what we were seeing.

Another major attraction is Blackjack's. This small sandwich shop situated by the public boat ramp directly on Lake Washington offers a delightful menu from which it is difficult to make a choice. The pulled pork is a tender, sauce-spiced, coleslaw-enhanced concoction served on a bun, and the square chicken sandwich is a perfectly grilled breast on square, white, buttery, toasted bread dressed with tomato, mayonnaise, and mustard. Blackjack's also serves a Philly and a variety of burgers. There are no tables inside, but a long padded bench near the takeout window makes waiting comfortable, and several tables are available on a pier that lets you dine on the water. Fishing, boating, and other water sports are the primary recreational activities in Glen Allan, but on a beautiful sunny day, with a good sandwich and a cold soft drink, it somehow seems quite enough.

Linden-on-the-Lake
1262 East Lake Washington Road
P.O. Box 99
Glen Allan, MS 38744
662-839-2181
Fax: 662-839-2182

From I-20, take Highway 61 north, go west on Highway 14, north on Highway 1 for 10 miles to Yazoo National Wildlife Refuge sign, west onto Refuge Road for 1 mile, then north onto East Lake Washington Road for 1/4 mile. Four rooms, one with private bath—other three share—in circa-1900 two-story National Register working cotton plantation home. Period furnishings. TV, phone available. Full Southern breakfast. Children over 5 only, no smoking, no pets. Reservation deposit required. Innkeepers Nancy and John Bridges. Rates $70-$85. Senior discount. AX, MC, V. Pays commission to travel agents.

Looking out over 8,500-acre Lake Washington, Linden stands on the highest point between Vicksburg and Greenville. Four massive fluted double columns reach to support a two-story front gallery.

Huge magnolias and oaks shade the front. The day we were there, owner John Bridges was cleaning up limbs that had been stripped from the trees in a recent ice storm. When we said something about the damage, Bridges replied, "I don't look at it as damage. It's God's pruning. Sometimes He has to take things in hand."

Bridges took us out to three shotgun houses on the north side of the brick mansion. Two of them were new and built from lumber salvaged by his son, a contractor in Jackson, from a project there. The first is divided into two suites and paneled in cypress—some boards more than two feet wide—that Bridges has sawn and planed in his own mill. The second of the two shotguns has been made into dormitory-type accommodations that are rented to duck hunters in season.

The third house is an original shotgun frame building that the innkeeper is restoring for use as a gift shop for his wife, who is a ceramist. Work is going on in the main house also. Bridges stated that even though he was taking guests, he was not really ready. Repainting and small repairs were under way inside and out.

One enters Linden into a wide main hallway with parlor on either side. Stairs on the left lead to the second floor, where the antique-furnished bedrooms are located.

GREENWOOD

Located on three rivers—the Yazoo, Tallahatchie, and Yalobusha—which flow in two directions, this Delta town of nearly 20,000 remains a bastion of cotton marketing, and from August until the end of the year, it is busy with the white fluff so important to its economy. Called the "Cotton Capital of the World," it celebrates with a "High Cotton Barbecue Cooking Contest" in April and "C. R. O. P. Day—Cotton Row on Parade" the first Saturday in August, honoring Greenwood's cotton marketing district. Traders have had offices on Front Street since the 1800s, and the area is now on the National Register of Historic Places.

With emphasis on cotton, the Cottonlandia Museum displays the history of Leflore County. Artifacts from the *Star of the West,* the first ship fired upon at Fort Sumter during the Civil War, and which is now buried in the Tallahatchie River, are exhibited here. The Malmaison Room features objects from the palatial home of Greenwood Leflore, the last chief of the Choctaws, including imported gold-finished French mahogany furniture upholstered in silk damask. This Native American planter and state senator named his house "Malmaison" after that of French empress Josephine.

Florewood River Plantation, two miles west of Greenwood and named for Leflore, recreates a 100-acre 1850s Mississippi Delta plantation and can be visited March through November; it also features a candlelight Christmas Tour.

Even though "cotton is still king" in Greenwood, as in other towns in this area many acres have been converted into catfish ponds, which can be seen along the highways. Several good restaurants are located here, and celebrations include the T-6 Formation Clinic and Airshow in May, the Mississippi International Balloon Classic in June, the 300 Oaks Road Race in September, Home in the Woods in Itta Bena in October, and the Delta Band Festival & Winter Carnival in December.

For more information, contact the Greenwood Convention and Visitors Bureau, 1902 Leflore Avenue, P.O. Drawer 739, Greenwood, MS, 1-800-748-9064 or 662-453-9197, www.netdoor.com/com/gcvb. They are open Monday-Friday from 9 to 5.

Bridgewater Inn
501 River Road
Greenwood, MS 38930
662-453-9265

*Four units—one suite and one room with private baths, two that
share a bath—in two-story 1910 Greek Revival home on the Yazoo
River. Antique furnishings. TV, phone. Kitchen privileges. Breakfast
may be ordered. Other meals by reservation. Tours, weddings, and special occasions. Children welcome, smoking on porches, no pets.
Reservation deposit required. Innkeeper Lucy Cooper. Rates $65-$85.
Senior and extended-stay discounts. AX, DS, MC, V.*

When we arrived at Bridgewater Inn, Mary Branch met us at
the door and invited us in. As she was showing us through the
house, we noticed that a tapestry hung in every room. This is
unique in our B&B experience. There were also stained-glass
windows and doors in this restored former rooming house.
Guests may use the totally renovated kitchen, as well as the rest
of the house. The bedrooms all have names—Yazoo, Regency,
Delta, and Lester Suite—and each one is decorated in a different color.

Mary is the mother of the owner of Bridgewater Inn, Lucy
Cooper, who is also a nurse in Jackson. Mary informed us that
Greenwood has a limousine service. The investors were originally told that the town was not big enough to support it. She
says that the owners like to use it for transportation to Jackson
to the wrestling matches, and it now does more business than
the bed and breakfast.

The Rivers' Inn
1109 River Road
Greenwood, MS 38930
662-453-5432
Fax: 662-453-9900

*Five rooms with three baths in circa-1912 New Orleans style home,
with antique ironwork, overlooking Yazoo River. Contemporary furnishings. Cable TV, phone, swimming pool. Full Southern breakfast.
Caters weddings, receptions, and business meetings. Children over 10
only, smoking restricted, no pets. Innkeeper Rose Marie Kennedy. Rates*

$65-$75. Senior discount, special group rates. AX, MC, V. Pays commission to travel agents.

Rose Marie Kennedy almost has a ghost story to go with the Rivers' Inn. Shortly after she purchased the place, she was awakened by a horrible clanging noise that seemed to be coming from the bathroom or the kitchen. She was afraid to leave her bedroom, and fortunately her mother slept through the commotion. Rose Marie told her neighbor about it the next day, and word soon got around that the original owner, a doctor with a taste for bourbon, was back and looking for his whiskey. A plumber, however, diagnosed water hammer caused by air buildup in the pipes.

Rose Marie says that she opened the Rivers' Inn in 1991 as Greenwood's first bed and breakfast, and it is located on historic River Road, once known as "Silk Stocking Avenue." Each of the guestrooms has a different-style decor, and she caters her full Southern breakfast, which is served in the light-filled sunrooms. She also caters weddings, rehearsals, reunions, and other social or business functions in her large party room overlooking the swimming pool, which guests may use.

HATTIESBURG

Hattie Hardy got a town named after her in 1882 by husband and Hattiesburg founder Capt. William H. Hardy. As did others, he came to south Mississippi to take advantage of the large stands of virgin longleaf pine here. The businessman also helped bring in the railroads that were so vital to a booming timber industry. As a result of these efforts, Hattiesburg became a hub for the industry. Even though it has a diversified economy today, it is still referred to as the "Hub City."

One of Hattiesburg's major assets is the University of Southern Mississippi, which provides a cultural and intellectual atmosphere on a beautiful campus. A large rose garden here is a major attraction. The city also has an excellent small zoo with tigers, lemurs, and a prairie-dog town.

Visitors who drive through the Historic District will see a variety of 19th- and early-20th-century buildings, including the

1928-29 Saenger Theatre, now a center for the performing arts. The Saenger's original Mahler pipe organ is still in use.

Outdoor activities are plentiful with canoeing and golfing heading the list. There are more than a dozen golf courses within a 30-mile radius. Timberton is the largest with 27 holes, and 18-hole Cane Brake is the newest. Okatoma Post and Black Creek Canoe Rentals offer trips from 3 to 19 miles, or a half-day, or overnighters up to three days.

Restaurants recommended to us include Chesterfield's and Purple Parrot. For additional information, contact the Hattiesburg Convention and Visitors Bureau, P.O. Box 16122, Hattiesburg, MS 39404-6122, 1-800-638-6877 or 601-268-3220.

Dunhopen Inn and Willows Fine and Casual Dining
3875 Veteran Memorial Drive
Hattiesburg, MS 39401
1-888-543-0707 or 601-543-0707
Fax: 601-543-0778
E-mail: info@dunhopen.com
Web site: www.dunhopen.com

Twelve rooms with private baths in a two-and-a-half-story replicated Federal Colonial-style home. Antique and reproduction furnishings. TV, phone, five whirlpools, four working fireplaces, swimming pool. Full breakfast. Restaurant serving dinner. Wine cellar. Receptions, weekend retreats, and corporate entertainment. No children, no smoking, no pets but will make veterinary referral. Credit card required for reservation. Innkeepers Candy James and Mike Ford. Rates $85-$150. All major credit cards.

*Dunhopen Inn
and Willows Fine
and Casual Dining*

From the moment we entered the front door to elegant Dunhopen Inn, we were hooked. This is definitely one of the finest properties we have visited, and even better, it encompasses a restaurant with a premium wine cellar. It also overlooks the ninth hole of Timberton Golf Club, a 27-hole course that hosts state championships and PGA events.

The units are named for outstanding Hattiesburg citizens, and each has its own color scheme and decor, but the overall theme is described as early American by innkeeper Candy James. The beds in the guestrooms are custom built in Massachusetts from specially selected woods—oak, cherry, and tiger maple—and one of the baths features a rare high-back clawfoot tub.

Dunhopen takes its name from a play on words. Owner and chef Mike Ford, brother to Candy, says everybody is "done hoping" now that the inn is a reality. It has been featured in *Mississippi* magazine, *In Mississippi Today,* and *Country Inns of America.*

Ford says that Willows brings "a new level of dining experience" to Hattiesburg and points out that his menu includes fresh smoked meats from his own smokehouse, along with offerings unusual for Mississippi—elk, pheasant, fish from the Pacific coast, ahi tuna, rack of lamb, and Black Angus beef from Montana. Both the wine list and dessert menu are extensive.

When reflecting on his decision to enter into a venture of this kind, Ford said, "I've always considered Hattiesburg home, and it is nice to bring something to life that just adds to our community."

HERNANDO

Named for Spanish explorer Hernando de Soto, this thriving north Mississippi town was founded in 1836, the same year that De Soto County came into being, on land ceded by the Chickasaw Indians. Edward Orne donated 40 acres to be used as a county seat, and 112 lots were laid out around the Courthouse Square. By 1839 there was a U.S. mail route from Holly Springs to Hernando. In 1856, the first train came through, on the Mississippi and Tennessee Railroad. It ran all the way from Memphis to Grenada.

Hernando's Classical Revival courthouse dates from 1940 and has been designated a Mississippi Landmark. Partly because of the urban sprawl of Memphis, Hernando has doubled its population since 1990. For more information, contact the De Soto County Convention and Visitors Center, 1-800-280-9120.

Magnolia Grove
140 East Commerce Street
Hernando, MS 38632
662-429-2626
Fax: 662-429-1585
Web site: www.magnoliagrove.com

Four rooms with private baths in two-story 100-year-old Greek Revival mansion. Antique furnishings. TV in room, phone available. Full gourmet breakfast. Dinner by reservation. Tours, weddings, showers, receptions, club activities, and photography sessions. No children, no smoking, no pets. Reservation deposit required. Innkeepers Robert and Phyllis Wolfe. Rates $100-$125. AX, DC, DS, MC, V.

Magnolia Grove is a magnificent four-columned, balconied Greek Revival home on a three-acre, tree-shaded lot including 13 magnolias, where innkeeper Phyllis Wolfe greets her guests with a warm welcome. She is not sure of the exact date of the house but is certain that it was built around a hundred years ago. It was purchased in 1902 by the Williams family, and in 1982 it was willed to Hernando United Methodist Church by their daughter, Ladye Eugenia Williams, upon her death at 92. In 1982, Mr. and Mrs. Fred Holmes bought the property and began restoration, and in 1997, Robert and Phyllis bought it and opened their bed and breakfast on March 1, 1998.

With 12-foot ceilings, hardwood floors, and lovely chandeliers, the home is tastefully furnished with antiques—some of which are family pieces—as well as stained glass. Each guestroom follows a distinct motif for its individual name. Visitors may stay in the Rose Room, Ladye Magnolia, Janie E., or Cole's Cottage and also have use of the parlors for relaxing.

Phyllis serves a full gourmet breakfast and provides dinner by reservation. She has self-published a cookbook entitled *Favorite*

Recipes from Magnolia Grove Bed and Breakfast, and we purchased a copy. One of her recipes is furnished below.

Breakfast Pizza

1 can crescent rolls
1 lb. Jimmy Dean sausage
1 onion, chopped
Shredded cheese (amount and type of your choice)
5 eggs
Salt and pepper to taste

Pat rolls into 9" x 13" baking dish. Brown meat with onion and drain. Spread over rolls. Sprinkle cheese over meat. Beat eggs; add salt and pepper and pour over cheese. Bake according to instructions on roll package (about 20 to 25 minutes).

Sassafras Inn Bed & Breakfast
785 Highway 51
Hernando, MS 38632
1-800-882-1897 or 662-429-5864
Fax: 662-429-4591
E-mail: sassyinn@mem.net
Web site: www.memphis.to

Located about two miles north of town. Four rooms with private baths in two-story brick contemporary home. Contemporary furnishings. Cable TV, VCP with free movies, phone, heated indoor pool, hot tub. Microwave, refrigerator, whirlpool in some rooms. Full Southern breakfast. Dinner by reservation. Children welcome, smoking restricted, no pets. Reservation deposit required. Seven-day cancellation policy. Innkeeper Francee McClanahan. Rates $65-$225, extra person $15. Corporate and senior discounts. AX, DS, MC, V. Pays commission to travel agents.

This is a contemporary property, the house having been built in 1985. Named for the sassafras trees that grow behind the house and the tea that energetic and friendly innkeeper Francee McClanahan serves, this bed and breakfast offers comfort and hospitality. From the heated indoor pool and adjacent hot tub, to the amenity-filled bathrooms, everything is arranged with the guests' comfort in mind.

Our upstairs room had a TV, VCP, CD player, sound machine, fresh fruit, soft drinks, candy, and snacks including home-baked cookies. There were robes to wear to the pool and swimsuits available for loan to guests who forget theirs. This room also has a skylight over the bed and is thus named the Skylight Suite. The eclectic yet tasteful furnishings include ample chairs, good lighting, and a comfortable bed.

Before we went to dinner, Francee informed us that if we had dessert we should be prepared to eat two. Sure enough, when we returned to our room, we heard a knock on the door, and upon answering it found a small table containing a tray with two large pieces of cake topped with a delicious white brandy-flavored cream sauce and a pot of coffee. Our breakfast was served the same way the following morning, and guests may request theirs in their rooms, in the dining room, or poolside. We have her recipe for Mock Eggs Benedict, which she serves with bacon, jelly-topped toast rounds, grits, juice, and coffee.

Mock Eggs Benedict

Slice an English muffin in half. Cut center out with a biscuit cutter and discard center. Place muffin ring in skillet on low heat with pat of butter in center. When warm, put poached egg gently into center of muffin. Top with hollandaise sauce and paprika.

HOLLY SPRINGS

Cotton was king in Holly Springs before the Civil War. During the war, U. S. Grant set up a supply depot here, but it was captured by Confederates and the supplies were destroyed. This small interesting city seems to have an antebellum home on every corner and three or four more in the middle of the block. The annual spring Pilgrimage, sponsored by the Holly Springs Garden Club, provides a chance for visitors to see some of these National Register homes as well as 1837 Hillcrest Cemetery and three antebellum churches—1849 First United Methodist, 1858 Christ Episcopal, and 1860 First Presbyterian. Montrose, built in 1858, is open by appointment throughout the year. *Golf Digest* rates the course at the Kirkwood National Golf Club as one of the top 50 in the United States, and Wall Doxey State Park and Chewalla Lake Recreation Area offer swimming and fishing. The Kudzu Festival in July is complete with a carnival, arts and crafts, entertainment, and barbecue contest.

For additional information, contact the Holly Springs Chamber of Commerce, 154 South Memphis Street, Holly Springs, MS 38635, 662-252-2943.

Somerset Cottage
135 West Gholson Avenue
Holly Springs, MS 38635
662-252-4513

One unit with private bath in circa-1860 guesthouse adjacent to two antebellum homes. Comfortably furnished. TV, phone, microwave, refrigerator. Continental breakfast. No children, no smoking, no pets. Reservation deposit required. Innkeeper Jean M. Liddy. Rates $65. No credit cards.

When Jean Liddy came to show us her property, we immediately suspected her accent. It turned out that she was a New Jersey native but that she had been in Holly Springs for 25 years. That probably makes her a Mississippian.

Jean's three-room cottage with bath contains a small sitting room, a comfortable bedroom with maple furnishings, including a queen-size feather bed, and a kitchen where she stocks a continental breakfast of coffee, juice, fruit, and pastry. She says, however, that she does not provide breakfast for guests who stay for an extended period.

On occasion, Jean caters next door, where her son and daughter-in-law have an 1863 two-story home with large magnolia trees in the front yard. Their Rutledge Carriage House in back was temporarily closed, but they hope to have it open to the public again soon. Jean also says a good lunch is available at the Kirkwood Golf Club.

IUKA

Hundreds of years ago, Chickasaw Indian chief Iuka discovered the mineral springs located in this hilly, remote area of

Mississippi, and the town was named for him. In the late 1800s people came from all around to enjoy the benefits of the healthful water, which was eventually bottled and even won first place at the 1904 World's Fair.

The sparkling natural elixir may still be tasted at the Iuka Mineral Springs Park. This facility is also an ideal area for bald eagles, and Eagle Tours are provided on the Tennessee River every January. Iuka's circa-1889 Tishomingo County Courthouse chronicles local history and contains Native American relics as well as artifacts from the 1862 Civil War Battle of Iuka. For golfers, the Iuka Country Club offers a semi-private nine-hole course.

East Port Inn Bed & Breakfast
100 South Pearl Street
Iuka, MS 38852
662-423-2511

Five rooms with private baths in circa-1864 two-story white frame house six miles from Pickwick Lake and near Shiloh National Military Park. Some antique furnishings. Cable TV, phone. Full Southern breakfast. Well-behaved children welcome, no smoking, no pets. Reservation deposit required. Innkeeper Betty Watson. Rates $40. Senior discount. AX.

Innkeeper Betty Watson stressed that she does not operate a "high end" bed and breakfast, but we found the inn to be comfortable and inviting with spacious guestrooms. Located on a relatively busy corner in old downtown Iuka, East Port Inn provides a handy spot for business and leisure travelers. Some of the furnishings are antique, but that is not the innkeeper's focus. Instead, she maintains an attractive property at very moderate prices.

Betty serves a full breakfast that includes eggs, grits, bacon or sausage, homemade biscuits, juice, coffee or tea, and occasionally her special cinnamon rolls.

JACKSON

The capital and largest city in the Magnolia State has at least two distinctions—it was named for Andrew Jackson, and it was burned by William Tecumseh Sherman. There was so little left when the Union general and his troops got through in 1863 that it was called "Chimneyville." Despite Sherman's best (or worst) efforts, Jackson survived, and today it is a thriving city of more than 200,000 people.

Mississippi centers around Jackson, geographically and economically, and the city draws tourists with a variety of cultural and historic attractions. The Mississippi Museum of Art contains works by Pierre-Auguste Renoir, Pablo Picasso, Georgia O'Keeffe, and important Mississippi artists. The Old State Capitol, started in 1833, completed in 1840, and replaced with a new building in 1903, now houses the State Historical Museum. The 1841 Governor's Mansion, still home to the state's first family, was headquarters for both Grant and Sherman during the Civil War. Restored Manship House, built in 1857, was the Gothic Revival home of Civil War mayor Charles Henry Manship.

Jackson hosts the Mississippi State Fair in early fall and a number of other special events and festivals throughout the year. A few miles west of town, southwesterly off I-20, the lower portion of the Natchez Trace Parkway winds down to Natchez. This scenic highway, maintained by the National Park Service, provides a delightful two-hour drive between the two cities.

For additional information, contact the Metro Jackson Convention and Visitors Bureau, 921 North President Street, P.O. Box 1450, Jackson, MS 39215, 1-800-354-7695 or 601-960-1891, www.visitjackson.com.

Fairview Inn
734 Fairview Street
Jackson, MS 39202
1-888-948-1908 or 601-948-3429
Fax: 601-948-1203
E-mail: fairview@fairviewinn.com
Web site: www.fairviewinn.com

Eight rooms with private baths in three-story palatial circa-1908 National Register mansion located just east of North State Street. Some antique furnishings. Cable TV, phone with computer dataport and voicemail, free movies, some whirlpools, meeting rooms. Full Southern

Fairview Inn

breakfast. Group dinners by reservation. Children welcome, no smoking, no pets. Credit card required for reservation. 72-hour cancellation policy. Innkeepers Carol and William Simmons. Rates $100-$165, extra person $15. AX, DC, DS, MC, V. Pays commission to travel agents.

At 20,000 square feet, Fairview Inn must certainly be one of the largest residential properties we have ever visited. Innkeeper Carol Simmons noted that the house had been in her husband's family since 1930. As she was showing us through, she said that the huge ballroom was the major modern addition and is capable of accommodating receptions or other events of up to a thousand people.

After taking us through the ground floor, from the elegant antique-filled parlor to the modern caterer's kitchen, Carol turned us over to Judy Fillingame, who showed us the upstairs guestrooms. Notable among these is the Hayloft Honeymoon Suite with a king-size bed and a spacious sitting area. The Executive Suite with its separate sitting room seems perfect for a businessperson on an extended stay.

Furnishings in the guest units are a pleasing mix of antiques and more modern pieces. The Natchez room even offers a Mallard bed, and the Carriage House Suite has a conference area. The house is Classic Greek Revival with eight columns supporting the front gallery. Six of these are Corinthian, and they are flanked by plain square supports on either end. Decks at the rear offer additional space for social functions when the weather is suitable.

Millsaps Buie House

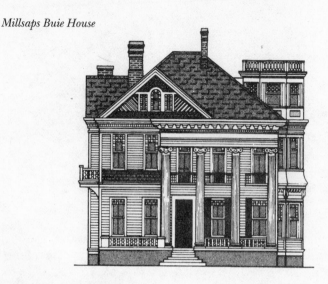

Millsaps Buie House
628 North State Street
Jackson, MS 39202
601-352-0221

Eleven rooms with private baths in elegant 1888 National Register Victorian mansion. Antique and period furnishings. TV, phone with computer dataport, fax machine available, some refrigerators. Delightful rooms, some 12-, some 14-foot ceilings, flowers, fruit, and turndown service. Full breakfast. Children over 12 only, no smoking, no pets. Reservations advised. Innkeeper Judy Fenter, associate innkeeper Harriet Brewer. Rates $85-$170, extra person $15. AX, DC, DS, MC, V. Pays commission to travel agents.

Millsaps Buie House is undoubtedly one of the finest inns in the South, from the standpoints of both service and accommodations. Their brochure says they are "a 19th century urban retreat for the 21st century traveler," and they most assuredly are elegantly so.

Located near downtown Jackson, with rooms that feature views of the state capitol, this late-19th-century jewel has original stained glass and hand-molded friezes and has been in the same family for five generations. Guests have the use of a drawing room, library, and parlor, as well as attractive grounds with brick walks. There is even a small conference room for business types, and free parking is ample.

The full breakfast here includes a hot casserole, cereal, muffin, fruit, juice, and coffee. Some bedrooms have refrigerators for the convenience of guests. Added touches include flowers, fruit, and nightly turndown service.

The Old Capitol Bed and Breakfast Inn
226 North State Street
Jackson, MS 39201
1-888-359-9001 or 601-359-9000
Fax: 601-355-5587
E-mail: inn@misnet.com
Web site: www.oldcapitolinn.com

Twenty-four units with private baths in three-story red-brick former YMCA building. Each room has different decor and furnishings. Cable TV, phone, swimming pool, off-street parking, snacks, wine, bicycles. Full Southern breakfast. No children, no smoking, no pets. Credit card required for reservation. Innkeeper Mende Malour. Rates $75-$145. DS, MC, V. Pays commission to travel agents.

It is certainly not like any YMCA we ever saw, but it is a remarkable property. With 24 guest units, the Old Capitol inn just barely fits within our criteria for inns; we usually use 25 as a max, and we are glad it made the cut.

Roan Evans was on the desk the Sunday afternoon that we showed up, and he did an excellent job giving us "the tour." This included the breakfast room, a bright, cheery spot that looked out over the patio, pool, and garden. He also showed us conference rooms, a coffee room, and a huge ballroom with a stage, draped with dark red curtains, which was once a basketball court.

All of the suites are nicely appointed with an eclectic mixture of antique and period furniture. Among those we checked was Faulkner's Flat, which held a typewriter and one of his books and was dedicated to the memory of the famous Oxford, Mississippi, author.

A story goes with the swimming pool. It was once, in its YMCA days, Olympic sized. In the remodeling it was shrunk to make more room for the backyard, which now includes pleasant sitting areas, a fountain, and small pond. Tables and chairs just outside the breakfast room make it possible to have the full Southern breakfast of eggs, grits, sausage, biscuits, juice, and coffee or tea served here.

At the top of the building we saw renovations being made to install a hot tub, deck, and small bar. Incidentally, this is one of three Jackson inns with elevators. In our experience, these are unusual amenities for B&Bs. With the ballroom and two conference rooms, the Old Capitol inn is able to host small seminars and light functions. Roan said that most of their customers stayed on weekdays, so weekends were usually quiet. A recent guest, he said, was Georgia's U.S. representative Newt Gingrich. Since the facility is near the center of the Mississippi state government complex, it is an excellent location for politicians.

Poindexter Park Inn
803 Deer Park
Mailing Address: 55 Nelson Circle
Jackson, MS 39212
601-944-1392
Fax: 601-948-3172

Six rooms with private baths in circa-1907 two-story frame structure. Eclectic and some antique furnishings. TV available, phone in room. Continental Plus breakfast. Children welcome, smoking outside, call about pets. Reservation deposit required. Innkeeper Marcia Weaver. Rates $59-$69. Senior and extended-stay discounts. AX, DS, MC, V. Pays commission to travel agents.

Poindexter Park Inn is now owned by a former Jackson councilwoman and is located in one of the city's oldest neighborhoods that today is a mix of industry and residences, predominantly African American. The property on which it stands was the George Poindexter Plantation and was owned by Mississippi's second governor, George Poindexter, who wrote the Mississippi Code. Poindexter Park is across the street from the inn, and Poindexter school and street are nearby.

Owner Marcia Weaver is a Jackson blues fan and has books,

Poindexter Park Inn

photographs, and other blues memorabilia in her home. She says that most people think Mississippi blues may be found only in the Delta, but one of the best blues clubs in Mississippi is right behind her house. Her brochure reads, "Blues Tour Starts at Poindexter Park Inn."

When Marcia bought the house it was almost gone, and she has a photo that was taken before she restored and renovated it. She has furnished it eclectically and has used quilts in a variety of ways—folded atop a bureau, for example. She also likes to use old luggage, and one piece serves as a lamp table.

Marcia usually serves fresh blueberry muffins with elderflower butter for breakfast and says she uses other edible flowers such as rose petals, pansies, oxalis, and daylilies for garnish and for the bath. She also says she will pick you up and deliver you to your plane or to other parts of the Natchez Trace.

LAKE CORMORANT (NESBIT)

We had a tough time with this location. Even though Bonne Terre Country Inn and Cafe has a Lake Cormorant mailing address, it is nearer to Nesbit, and the people in Hernando tend to claim it. When we got there we could see why.

Bonne Terre Country Inn
and Cafe

Bonne Terre Country Inn and Cafe
4715 West Church Road
Lake Cormorant, MS 38641
662-781-5100
Fax: 662-781-5466
Web site: www.bonneterre.com

Two-room suite and 12 rooms with private baths in white two-story Greek Revival style home located on 100 acres in Mississippi Highlands. French and English country antique furnishings. TV, phone available. Fishing on two lakes; walking trails; wildlife; conference center; swimming pool; fresh flowers; fireplaces; hot tubs; masseuse services; balconies or porches overlooking lake, pecan grove, or wildflower gardens. Gourmet breakfast and other meals served in adjacent restaurant. Retreats, meetings, weddings, picnics, fall hayrides. Children welcome, no smoking, no pets. Reservation deposit required. Innkeepers Max and June Bonnins. Rates $135-$185. AX, MC, V.

Since Lake Cormorant was the address we had, we drove there looking for Bonne Terre, but it was someplace else. Drive about five miles north of Hernando on I-55 and turn left at the second four-way stop (Church Road). Go about three miles and look for a small sign at a white-fenced driveway on the left. About 1/4 mile over an unpaved road, you will find this magnificent establishment.

We had reservations for dinner and were directed to the

restaurant as soon as we parked the car. After being seated by the maitre d' in a dining room filled with candlelit tables covered with white cloths and surrounded by windows overlooking the lake (even though it was dark, and we could not see it, for which our white-coated waiter apologized), we knew that we were in for a treat. We were not wrong. We had a choice of a three- or four-course meal but opted for the three.

After a glass of Merlot, we had hors d'oeuvres of smoked salmon with cream-cheese sauce sent us by the French chef, and Jack ordered steamed mussels with garlic sauce, arugula salad with kalamata olives in a light dressing, and medallions of venison in chocolate sauce with pears and parsnips. Winnie had lobster bisque, Bonne Terre salad (new potatoes, bacon bits, and endive with a warm dressing), Cajun sautéed catfish with turnip greens and sautéed small, flat, whole onions. We both had rolls and cornbread, but neither of us had room for dessert.

After dinner, owner Max Bonnins interrupted his meal to give us a tour of his two-story Bonne Terre ("good earth"), and this was another pleasurable experience. He told us that he and wife June opened their French-style country inn and restaurant in 1996 in order to provide a place where people could relax and escape the daily stress of hectic lives. All of the tastefully decorated rooms are furnished with French and English antiques and hot tubs, and those upstairs have balconies, while the ones downstairs have porches for relaxing and taking in the beautiful lake and countryside. Rooms have names, some of them descriptive, such as Camellia, Chestnut, Francesca, Jasmine, Magnolia, Rowe, Sage, Wedgwood, and Willow.

LAUREL

Laurel began life in 1882 as a lumber camp when the Southern Pacific Railroad put a line through and lumber companies from Iowa came down to take advantage of the timber. Eleven years later, Eastman-Gardiner & Company established the first giant mill. Others followed and by the 1900s, the town was the largest producer of yellow pine in the world. With John Lindsey's invention of the eight-wheeled wagon in 1899 and William Mason's discovery of a process to make hardboard from mill waste in 1926, the industry grew and kept growing. Today timber production remains one of the two largest industries in Laurel, the other being oil.

The town's Historic District, with the largest intact group of early-20th-century architecture in the state, is listed on the National Register of Historic Places. The homes in the district are Craftsman Style, adopted by Frank Lloyd Wright and others. Usually, no architects were used; carpenters and contractors either suggested designs or built according to the owner's wishes. Low, horizontal lines, porches with squat columns, and exposed rafters along the eaves characterize the style.

The oldest house in Jones County, the circa-1840 Deason House, is located in Ellisville just a few miles south. Built of hand-hewn heart pine, the home has an unusual hexagonal entrance. It was here that army deserter Newt Knight, who ran with a gang of Jayhawkers in Jones County, murdered Confederate major Amos McLemore in 1863.

Attractions include Landrum's Country Homestead and Village and Trapper's Gator Farm. Landrum's, located about three miles south on Highway 15, is a re-creation of a late 1800s settlement complete with general store, cabins, jail, chapel, and gristmill. In addition to alligators, Trapper's has a bear, cougars, deer, foxes, and turtles.

The Lauren Rogers Museum of Art was the first of its kind in Mississippi. Located in the Historic District, it has more than 2,000 items in its permanent collection, including 19th-century European art, 19th- and 20th-century American art, English Georgian silver, Japanese woodblock prints, and Native American baskets.

Laurel Inn
803 North Second Avenue
Laurel, MS 39440
601-428-8773

Three units with private baths in two-story 1917 home in Historic District. Eclectic furnishings. TV, phone. Full Southern breakfast. Other meals by request. Weddings, receptions, and special events. Children welcome, smoking outside, no pets. Innkeepers Kevin and Peggy O'Connell. Rates $85. AX, MC, V. Pays commission to travel agents.

Laurel Inn

When we visited this bed and breakfast, Kevin and Peggy O'Connell had recently purchased it. Peggy said that she and Kevin had stayed here, fallen in love with the old house, and told the previous owner, Lucy Hogan Otto, that if she ever decided to sell the inn, they would like to buy it. She told them it was for sale, and they bought it and moved here from New Orleans to begin operation. Among the O'Connells' guests have been Vicki Lawrence, Delta Burke, and Gerald McRaney, but Peggy's two lively grandsons, Dakota and Blake, were her guests the Sunday afternoon that we visited Laurel Inn.

Timber baron John Murray Bissell built this Colonial Revival style clapboard home in 1917. Heart pine, personally selected by Bissell, was used for construction, and in all of the 5,400-square-foot building, there is said to be only one knot, which Peggy says she cannot find. The exterior is symmetrical, a feature of Colonial Revival. For example, if you drew a line down the middle of the main house, you would discover that the front door and its semi-elliptical arch are perfectly centered, as is the window above, with left and right windows providing exact balance.

The interior is elegant with intricate architectural designs, hand-pegged bookcases, and built-in china cabinets. The parlor features an Adam-style fireplace and mantel decorated with swags and daisies. The guest accommodations are elegant and comfortable with spacious bathrooms, although one is not *en suite* but directly across the hall.

LONG BEACH

If it were not for the signs, you would be hard put to tell when you left Pass Christian and entered Long Beach. Like its next-door neighbor, it is full of elegant old summer homes built by New Orleanians trying to get away from the heat and humidity of the city. At Hardy Hall on the University of Southern Mississippi Gulf Park campus, you will find the venerable Friendship Oak, a 500-year-old live oak that is 50 feet tall and has a limb spread of 151 feet. According to the story, those who stand in its shadow remain friends for life.

For restaurants in Long Beach, try Chappy's, which adds wild game, veal, and lamb to the usual coastal fare of seafood and steak. Chimney's is another good choice for seafood, and since it is located at the small-craft harbor, you get the additional pleasure of watching the boats while you eat. The Carnival Association of Long Beach hosts a Mardi Gras celebration each year.

Red Creek Inn, Vineyard, and Racing Stable
7416 Red Creek Road
Long Beach, MS 39560
1-800-729-9670 or 228-452-3080
Fax: 228-452-3080
E-mail: info@redcreekinn.com
Web site: www.redcreekin.com

Seven rooms with five baths in 1899 French-style raised cottage. Antique furnishings. TV available, phone available. Full breakfast. Children welcome, no smoking, call about pets. Reservation deposit required. Innkeepers Karl and Toni Mertz. Rates $40-$140. Senior discount. No credit cards, but takes personal checks. Pays commission to travel agents.

Red Creek Inn, established in 1986, was the first bed and breakfast inn on the Mississippi Gulf Coast, of which Karl and Toni Mertz are quite proud. Set in the countryside a few miles north of the beaches, it is also a place where Karl keeps his Thoroughbred racehorses, which have run at Hoosier Park in Indianapolis and at Delta Downs in Vinton and Evangeline Downs in Lafayette (both in Louisiana). His horse won in Indiana on his and Toni's wedding day.

*Red Creek Inn,
Vineyard, and
Racing Stable*

The Mertzes' three-story brick and cypress home is situated on 12 acres dotted with magnolias and live oaks. In fact, one of the oaks is named "Friendship, Too," and is registered with the Live Oak Society. The house has six fireplaces, and there are swings on the 64-foot front porch. The Victorian Room, which is the inn's honeymoon suite, has a marble whirlpool as well as a four-poster queen-size bed, triple dresser, and highboy. The French and Country Rooms are in the attic with a bunkroom located between them, making the entire setup ideal for families with children. There is also a sleeping porch, and Freedman's Quarters is located on the ground floor.

Karl Mertz says that he grew up commuting between Mendham, New Jersey, and Long Beach, but his adult life was spent in and around Atlanta. Toni (Maria Antonia Martinez) was born in Mexico but reared in Illinois. Karl also says that besides being yard boy for the inn, he is a graduate of Perkinston Junior College, the University of Southern Mississippi, Emory University, and Vanderbilt University. Toni graduated from Atlanta School for Floral Design and was working as a designer when she and Karl met. The couple have four sons, now grown.

Karl collects anecdotes about his guests. As he tells it, "Two sisters from Germany were standing on our front porch looking at the seedpods from the magnolia tree, and one asked, 'Is that a pineapple tree?'"

And, "I had a New Yorker wanting me to teach him (the guest) how to drive the lawn tractor, and then he asked if I would mind if he mowed the 12-acre front yard."

While we were standing on the front porch, Karl said, "Look out for the Mississippi state bird—the mosquito."

The breakfast at Red Creek is full, and we have one of Karl's recipes.

Big Shrimp Omelet

6 eggs
1 tbsp. butter, melted
1 tbsp. finely chopped green onion
1 tsp. finely chopped parsley
⅓ cup additional butter
¼ lb. peeled, cleaned, freshly boiled small shrimp
More finely chopped green onions
Salt
Pepper
Garlic salt
American cheese (optional)

In a medium bowl beat eggs thoroughly and add 1 tbsp. melted butter and 1 tbsp. green onions. Add parsley and mix lightly. In a warm cast-iron frying pan, combine the egg mixture with remaining ⅓ cup butter. Increase the heat slightly and roll mixture over, decrease the heat, and continue to cook. As the softness disappears add the shrimp, green onions, and seasonings. If cheese is added, omit most of the garlic salt. Serve with homegrown sliced tomatoes and freshly baked bread, rolls, and homemade jam. Serves two.

LORMAN

Located about 12 miles south of Port Gibson, Lorman is in the middle of plantation country, but the land that was once planted with rows of cotton is now filled with rows of Christmas trees, even though you still see the occasional acreage of white fluff if you go in the early fall. The Civil War "Battle of the Bales" was fought here, and Rosswood Plantation was used as a hospital for wounded Union and Confederate soldiers.

Once a thriving farming town, Lorman has obviously seen better days. Even the old General Store, which tried to make the transition to an upscale restaurant, has given up the ghost, at least for the present. However, no one can take away Lorman's position as the place where *El Camino Real* met the Natchez Trace. It was at Lorman that the Spanish Highway ended, after beginning in Mexico City, and the Trace began snaking its way up through Mississippi and into Tennessee.

Canemount Plantation
Route 2, Box 45
Lorman, MS 39096
1-800-423-0684 or 601-877-3784
Fax: 601-877-2010

Nine units with private baths in four antebellum structures on 10,000-acre plantation. Antique furnishings. TV in sunroom, phone available, heated swimming pool. Hiking, fishing, hunting packages. Full breakfast and dinner. Children over 12 only, smoking outside, no pets. Reservation deposit required. Innkeepers Ray and Rachel Forrest. Rates $195-$225. MC, V.

You must visit Canemount Plantation to believe it. This amazing property gives you the run of 10,000 acres where wild turkeys, whitetail deer, and Russian boars roam at will. Your accommodations will be in one of four antebellum structures, which include the Pond House, the Grey Cottage, Rick's Cottage, and the Carriage House. The main house is an 1855 Italianate Revival marvel.

The Pond House was originally the home of the builders of Canemount, the Murdochs, and it is located just behind the main house by a fish-stocked pond. The Grey Cottage is a restored slave cabin with fireplace and whirlpool. The Carriage House is a restored barn with six minisuites, each containing a fireplace and wet bar. It is often used for corporate retreats with fax and telephone available.

Breakfast is served in the sunroom, where Wilma Green makes delicious blueberry pancakes and other breakfast goodies. After the meal, Rachel will give you a tour of the main house. In the evening, guests are offered a Safari Tour to historic sites not open to the general public and to see some of the

animals that abound on the property. When you return from
the tour, cocktails and dinner are waiting at "The Persnickety
Pig," an old dairy barn now transformed into a dining room.
Louisiana-trained chef James Coco creates the evening meal,
which features such entrees as grilled salmon and prime rib.

James was chef at the Old Country Store, which has recently
closed. The Cohn brothers established this old building in 1875
as a general store, which it remained until 1995. The old store
building is still standing but is no longer open to the public.

At Canemount, the Forrests will arrange bow hunts for you
on the plantation that has one of the finest deer herds in
Mississippi. Rates for a four-day hunt, including accommodations and all meals, are $1,780 per person with a bag limit of
one trophy buck plus a doe a day and one boar if you are lucky.
Guided-only three-day Russian boar hunts are priced at $1,200
per person.

The bream- and bass-stocked ponds are available for fishing,
and John Forrest, son of the owners, took a world record bream
from one on a fly rod. You should bring your own tackle, however.

On our visit to Canemount we stayed in the Grey Cottage,
home of Ben Coleman, once a slave here and now the resident
ghost. He lived here all his life, as did his son Paul, later.

Among the historical sites on the Canemount property are
the Windsor Ruins, whose 23 lonely Corinthian columns are
all that hauntingly remain of a once-proud mansion.

When it came time for our Safari Tour, guide James Allement
loaded us into a white Suburban and we took off across field and
wood to see the sights and spot the animals. James soon braked
at the edge of an open area with fairly heavy forest as a backdrop.

"Deer," he said, pointing. Sure enough, there were four
whitetails grazing just in front of the tree line. He handed us
the binoculars and said, "Look behind the front four and you
will see three more, one lying down and two standing."

Through the course of the hour-and-a-half ride we saw 20 to
30 deer, a dozen or more boars, several flocks of turkeys, two
armadillos, and a rabbit. James then delivered us to the
Persnickety Pig, where Chef Coco was waiting.

The menu that night consisted of a spicy appetizer of seared venison tenderloin with artichoke hearts and ancho chili peppers, followed by a salad of mixed baby greens and tomato dressed with asparagus vinaigrette. The entree was pork tenderloin with Italian mayonnaise, and for dessert the talented chef served homemade vanilla ice cream with blueberry sauce. At Coco's recommendation we chose a young Chilean cabernet sauvignon to accompany the meal.

Breakfast was at 9 the next morning, Wilma decided that we would have her Southwestern Scrambled Skillet, which she served with orange juice and coffee. James and Wilma generously shared some recipes with us that are included below.

Seared Venison Tenderloin with Artichoke Hearts and Ancho Chili Peppers
(James Coco)

1 can artichoke hearts, quartered
3 ancho chili peppers (smoked jalapenos), sliced
¼ stick butter
1 tbsp. sweet Thai chili sauce
Venison tenderloin

Combine all ingredients except venison and simmer 15 minutes. Remove silver skin and membrane from tenderloin and season with salt and pepper. Sear in medium-hot, dry skillet on all sides, slice thinly, and place around artichoke and ancho.

Asparagus Vinaigrette
(James Coco)

¼ lb. fresh asparagus tips
¼ cup rice-wine vinegar
¼ cup apple-cider vinegar
Pinch dill
Pinch basil
½ cup extravirgin olive oil

Cook asparagus until tender, drain, and cool. Combine all ingredients except oil, and puree in blender. Add oil slowly, and blend 1 minute.

Southwestern Scrambled Skillet
(Wilma Green)

1 lb. pan sausage
1 large white potato cubed
1 large onion, chopped
1 large green pepper, chopped
1 stalk celery, chopped
Dash cayenne pepper
4 eggs
1 cup shredded Monterey Jack or cheddar cheese
Salsa, warmed
Sour cream
8 corn tortillas, steamed

Brown sausage and fry potatoes in separate skillets, preferably cast iron. Add onions, green pepper, celery, and cayenne pepper to sausage and cook until vegetables are soft. Add potatoes and cook for 10 minutes. Fry eggs while mixture is cooking. Divide sausage mix onto 4 warm plates, and top with cheese, egg, salsa, and a good dollop of sour cream. Serve with corn tortillas. Serves four.

Sausage Quiche
(Wilma Green)

1 lb. pan sausage
1 medium onion, chopped
2 tbsp. flour
1 cup shredded cheddar
1 unbaked pie shell
4 eggs, beaten
1 cup half-and-half
Chopped parsley and green pepper rings for garnish

Brown sausage and onion in skillet. Cook until onion is soft. Stir in flour. Sprinkle ½ cup cheddar in bottom of pie shell. Add sausage mixture and remaining cheese. Combine eggs and half-and-half and pour over all. Bake 25 minutes at 350 degrees or until set. Garnish with parsley and pepper rings. Serves four to six.

Rosswood Plantation

Rosswood Plantation
Route 1, Box 6
Lorman, MS 39096
1-800-533-5889 or 601-437-4215
Fax: 601-437-6888
E-mail: whylander@aol.com
Web site: www.rosswood.net

Located on State Road 552, two and one-half miles east of Highway 61. Four rooms with private baths in two-story 1857 National Register Mississippi Landmark home on working plantation. Antique furnishings. TV, VCP with free movies, phone, heated pool, whirlpool. Stocked fishing pond, hiking trails, gift shop. Full Southern breakfast. Other meals by prior arrangement. Call about children, smoking in designated areas, no pets. Reservation required. Five-day cancellation policy. Innkeepers Jean and Walt Hylander. Rates $115-$135, extra person $25. AX, DS, MC, V. Pays commission to travel agents.

Rosswood Plantation home is an 1857 Classical Greek Revival built by David Shroeder, the Windsor architect. The diary of the first owner, Dr. Walter Ross Wade, reveals tales of ghosts, buried treasure, and slave revolts. At its height, Rosswood was a thriving 1,250-acre cotton plantation where more than 100 slaves toiled in the fields. Now it contains 100 acres filled with deer and other wildlife.

Rosswood's 14 rooms have 14-foot ceilings, and there are 10 fireplaces, Ionic-columned upper and lower galleries, and original slave quarters. The four guestrooms, located upstairs in the mansion, feature antique furnishings, canopied bed, down comforters, and a coffee and tea tray before the full breakfast is served in the main dining room.

The inn is popular with couples for weddings, honeymoons, and anniversaries. It offers swimming, fishing, hunting, biking, hiking, birdwatching, and sight-seeing. As you approach the mansion from the highway, a serene pond on the left is surrounded by scores of Christmas-tree-shaped cedars. When we arrived, Jean and Walt Hylander were busy with incoming and outgoing guests and invited us to join the ongoing tour. So we fell in behind the couple checking in and followed Walt and the guests upstairs, where we got a look at all the rooms.

LULA (DUNDEE)

The inn described below is actually located on Moon Lake, a beautiful body of water just a few miles off Highway 49 and near the Mississippi River and Arkansas. It is closer to the Lula community, but it has a Dundee mailing address.

Uncle Henry's Place Bed and Breakfast
5860 Moon Lake Road
Dundee, MS 38626
662-337-2757

Uncle Henry's Place Bed and Breakfast

Five rooms, three with private baths and two that share, in a circa-1926 structure built by the Elks Club of Clarksdale, Mississippi. Eclectic furnishings, some family pieces. TV in room, phone available. Fishing and boating. Full Southern breakfast. Restaurant available for other meals. Children welcome, no smoking, no pets. Reservation deposit required. Innkeeper Sarah B. Wright. Rates $65. MC, V. Pays commission to travel agents.

Uncle Henry's Place was known as the Moon Lake Club in the 1930s and operated as a casino before it was bought by Henry Trevino in 1946. It is mentioned in all of Tennessee Williams' works but two, and William Faulkner also refers to it. Both were probably visitors.

Today the facility is filled with family memorabilia and furniture and operated by Sarah B. Wright, who was reared by Henry and his wife, Vedah. Sarah says that she came to live here when her own parents died, and when she got the property she changed the name to Uncle Henry's because that was what she always called Trevino.

The rooms each have two names. The earlier, or official, names deal with gambling, so now the Blackjack Room is also the Confederate Room, and the Deuces Wild Room is the Pink Room—and so it goes. Incidentally, the Pink Room once had a buzzer to warn of impending raids by police against illegal betting operations.

What was at one time an open balcony on the second floor is now enclosed to make a large common area that looks out over the lake. Downstairs are a restaurant and a party room called the Jitterbug Room. Here, guests may listen to oldies on the jukebox and twirl on the large dance floor if they so desire. The restaurant features many seafood items such as Broiled Catfish Stuffed with Crabmeat, Crabmeat au Gratin, and Soft-Shell Henry.

NATCHEZ

Looking down from its high bluff to the Mississippi River, Natchez is the "Old South" personified. Established by Bienville in 1716 as Fort Rosalie, the town served time under the English and Spanish as well as under the French and takes its present name from the Natchez Indians. Its heyday came in with cotton near the turn of the 19th century and lasted until the Civil War. Natchez remains filled with magnolias, mansions, and moonlight.

With more than 500 historic buildings, Natchez truly reflects the plantation era in American history. In the 60 years prior to the Civil War, cotton was king here, and the town became a major shipping point for the commodity. It was during this period that most of the magnificent mansions that the visitor sees today were built. Throughout the centuries that the town has existed, French, English, Spanish, Confederate, and United States flags have flown over it. Famous people have walked Natchez streets, including Mark Twain, Henry Clay, Aaron Burr, Andrew Jackson—even Marie Joseph Paul Yves Roch Gilbert du Motier, Marquis de Lafayette.

However, Natchez had two faces. In addition to wealth and genteel society on the bluffs was Natchez-Under-the-Hill, a rip-roaring river port below, where thieves and sailors mixed with gamblers and prostitutes. Saloons and brothels lined the streets, and fights and killings were common. Caves were dug into the hillsides to hide stolen merchandise, and they were partially responsible for the demise of this infamous area. The digging caused landslides in the erosion-prone brown loess that comprises the bluffs. Under-the-Hill was eventually abandoned. Today, some of the buildings have been restored and converted to shops and restaurants, and riverboat casinos now dock here.

An economic slump following the Civil War contributed to the preservation of the old buildings, and the town is filled with architectural gems unparalleled in America. Natchez celebrates this heritage with two annual pilgrimages, one in March/April and the other in October. Many of the antebellum homes are open to the public, and it takes a three-day visit to see them all. Each tour features five houses, and there are two tours a day.

As you would expect in a town that attracts a lot of visitors, there are many places to eat, and Natchez innkeepers will usually make recommendations and reservations. A wide variety of food is available, but the accent is on Southern cooking. Baked ham and fried chicken are two of the specialties at the Carriage House Restaurant and Lounge on the grounds of Stanton Hall, and the okra and seafood gumbo is a good lunch choice at Magnolia Grill Under-the-Hill. King's Tavern, in the oldest building in the territory, prides itself on its steak, but also offers shrimp and baked catfish.

Brothers features daily specials and produces good sandwiches in a casual atmosphere. Natchez Landing, another Under-the-Hill spot, has barbecue, steak, catfish, and shrimp. There are others, but these are some that we have tried and liked.

For further information, contact the Natchez Convention and Visitor Bureau, 311 Liberty Road, Natchez, MS 39120, 1-800-647-6724 or 601-446-6345.

Reservations for many of the Natchez bed and breakfasts can be made through Natchez Pilgrimage Tours. Their toll-free telephone number is 1-800-647-6742.

The Briars Inn
31 Irving Lane
P.O. Box 1245
Natchez, MS 39121
1-800-634-1818 or 601-446-9654
Fax: 601-442-1290

The Briars Inn
Illustation by Donald Standich

On a point overlooking the river and reached through the Ramada Inn parking area. Fifteen rooms with private baths in 1814 plantation-style National Register home and nearby guesthouse. Antique and reproduction furnishings. Cable TV, phone. Hairdryers, fireplaces, screened swimming pool. Tour included. Full Southern breakfast. Children over 12 only, no smoking in bedrooms, no pets. Reservation deposit required. 14-day cancellation policy; cancellation fee charged. Innkeepers Robert E. Canon and Newton Wilds. Rates $140-$155, extra person $50. AX, MC, V. Pays commission to travel agents.

The plantation-style architecture of the Briars is believed to have been the work of Philadelphian Levi Weeks. Ten slim Doric columns parade across the 80-foot veranda, and the 48-foot drawing room features twin staircases and Palladian arches. Before a carved-wood, Adam-style mantel in the parlor, in 1845, Jefferson Davis married his second wife, Varina Howell, in a simple ceremony. His first wife, a daughter of Zachary Taylor, had died of yellow fever. At the time of the Briars wedding, Kentucky-born Davis was on the threshold of a spectacular political career; he would become a U.S. senator from Mississippi, secretary of war, and finally, president of the Confederate States of America.

Today, the mansion's 19 acres of rolling hills provide a delightful landscaped panorama of woods, camellias, azaleas, and excellent overlooks of the mighty Mississippi. There are separate guest quarters with river views and a dining pavilion where the full plantation breakfast is served. Morning coffee is available on the main-house veranda, public rooms are open to guests around the clock, and the screened swimming pool is a pleasant place to unwind on a summer day.

The Burn Mansion
712 North Union Street
Natchez, MS 39120
1-800-654-8859 or 601-442-1344
Fax: 601-445-0606

Located in heart of Historic District. Seven units with private baths in 1834 Greek Revival National Register home and adjacent garçonnière.

Antique furnishings. TV in main-house rooms, phone available, swimming pool. Tour included. Full breakfast. Complimentary beverages. Children welcome, smoking on patio, no pets. Reservation deposit required. Seven-day cancellation policy. Innkeeper Layne Taylor. Rates $120-$200, extra person $30. AX, DS, MC, V. Pays commission to travel agents.

The Burn Mansion, which appears to be a one-and-a-half-story cottage from the front, is actually three stories and served as a Union hospital during the siege of Vicksburg. Built in 1834 by John P. Walworth, wealthy planter and merchant, the Greek Revival mansion is set on four and one-half acres of gardens, fountains, and statuary. Doric columns grace the front portico, and interior furnishings include a Mallard bed, Empire dining table, Aubusson carpet, and Belgian draperies. The cottage features Eastlake furniture. Rooms are named for the original family: Sarah, Lucy, Walworth, Douglas, Clara, Renee, and Laura.

Since it was one of Natchez's first Greek Revival homes, the Burn is known as "the transition house of Natchez," according to owner Layne Taylor. When Walworth had it built on 100 acres within the city limits, the Burn was the largest private estate inside the town. Even though most of the acreage is gone, the home itself remains the largest private residence here with more than 11,000 square feet of interior floor space.

The Burn, as early Scots settlers would call a stream, takes its name from a now nonexistent brook that ran through the property. The house remained in the Walworth family until the 1940s, when Ernestine, the last of three generations of Walworths, died.

A full plantation breakfast is served in the formal dining room, and guests may enjoy complimentary evening cocktails. Rockers and wicker furniture on porches and in courtyards invite visitors to relax, as does the swimming pool. An herb garden provides seasonings for the kitchen, and 125 varieties of camellias bloom profusely in season. The Burn does special candlelight dinners for parties of 24 or more, and an extensive menu is available.

Coyle House

Coyle House
307 South Wall Street
Natchez, MS 39120
601-445-8679

Two suites with private baths in 1793-94 National Register raised cottage. Antique furnishings, family pieces. TV, phone. Private entrance. Off-street parking. Full Southern breakfast. Children over 8 only, no smoking in rooms, no pets. Reservation required. Innkeepers Mr. and Mrs. Roger Smith. Rates $120, extra person $30. MC, V. Pays commission to travel agents.

According to the Roger Smiths, the current owners, Coyle House was one of the first homes to be built on the bluff in Natchez's Spanish section. Almost everything else was under the hill. Surveyor Hugh Coyle built the raised cottage but was seldom here. He was in Louisiana surveying much of Rapides Parish and other areas.

The Smiths bought the house in 1994 from the Natchez Historical Society and restored it to its present pristine condition, after Roger had worked for International Paper Company for 38 years. Both suites have private entrances with off-street parking, are comfortably furnished, and feature huge bathrooms, each the size of a bedroom, which is what they were before renovation. One has a whirlpool and the other a shower.

Breakfast at Coyle House is full Southern—grits, sausage, eggs, biscuits, preserves, fruit, juice, and coffee or tea. The Smiths say quite a few Australian guests find their way here, and most of their visitors enjoy being within walking distance of nearly everything.

Dorsey House
305 North Pearl Street
Natchez, MS 39120
1-800-695-5845 or 601-442-5845
Fax: 601-442-1241

Two rooms and a suite with private baths in 1835 National Register townhouse. Period furnishings. TV in suite, phone available. Full Southern breakfast. Children welcome, no smoking, no pets. Innkeeper Brenda Edgin. Rates $130-$160. MC, V. Pays commission to travel agents.

Innkeeper Brenda Edgin greeted us at the door of Dorsey House and explained that it was Gloria's day off. Gloria is the housekeeper and the person who makes Dorsey House work, according to the owner.

There is one guestroom on the ground floor, and its bath is not *en suite*. It is reserved for this room only, but it is located down the hall past the kitchen. Brenda said that this has never been a problem, but she is always careful to explain the situation to potential guests.

The other two units are on the second floor, and the Edgins' private quarters are one more flight up. Breakfast, prepared and served by the indomitable Gloria, may be scrambled eggs, sausage or ham, butter or cheese grits, biscuits, preserves, fruit, juice, and coffee or tea.

Dunleith
84 Homochitto Street
Natchez, MS 39120
1-800-433-2445 or 601-446-8500
(Also available through Natchez Pilgrimage Tours)

Eleven guestrooms with private baths in 1856 white-columned Greek Revival National Historic Landmark. Antique furnishings. TV, phone. Conference facilities, working fireplaces. Tour included. Full breakfast. Complimentary lemonade, snack baskets in room. No children, no smoking, no pets. Innkeeper Nancy Gibbs. Rates $95-$140. DS, MC, V.

Dunleith
Illustration by
Rubia Sherry

With 26 stately white pillars surrounding antebellum Dunleith, it is the only fully colonnaded home in Mississippi, and a wrought-iron fence encloses the 40 acres on which it stands. Also featuring double galleries and a courtyard wing, the mansion has been called the most photographed house in America.

The interior is filled with 18th- and 19th-century furnishings, many from France. Ceiling medallions and 12 mantels are original, and carpets were custom made in Puerto Rico. The dining-room wallpaper was printed from 1855 wood blocks sometime before World War I and hidden in a cave in Alsace-Lorraine for protection during the war. This resulted in small mildew stains, which can still be seen.

Three of the elegant accommodations are in the main house, and the others in the wing. Guests may explore the gardens and grounds along brick and gravel paths, and take breakfast in a cheerful brick and wood-paneled converted poultry house topped with a *pigeonnier.*

Elgin
#1 Elgin Plantation Road
Natchez, MS 39120
601-446-6100
(Also available through Natchez Pilgrimage Tours)

Three rooms with two and one-half baths in 1853 National Register guest house of 1792 property. Antique and other furnishings. TV, phone. Full Southern breakfast. Call about children, smoking on galleries, no pets. Reservation deposit required. Innkeeper Ruth Ellen Calhoun. Rates $95-$150, extra person $20. No credit cards. Pays commission to travel agents.

Elgin

We sat in one of the first two rooms built by the Dunbar family at Elgin and looked through the wavy glass panes at the original slender-columned front porch that is now on the side of the house. Owner Ruth Ellen Calhoun told us Dr. John Carmichael Jenkins bought the place and added the rooms from 1840 into the 1850s. She noted that the attached building, which houses her guests, was constructed in 1853 and that it does not match the big house architecturally. That is because Jenkins built it as a replica of his uncle's guesthouse in Cold Springs, near Woodville, where Jenkins had lived as a young man. His uncle was Dr. John Carmichael, and Jenkins received a considerable inheritance from him.

A noted pioneer horticulturist, Jenkins married Annie Dunbar when she was 19 and he was older. Unfortunately, they both died of yellow fever a few years later. The Calhouns have diaries left by Jenkins, and copies are available for guests to read. In one of them, he mentions the "new house" that he is building. Today the two-story brick guest quarters has a large sitting/dining room downstairs and three bedrooms and two baths upstairs. The main house and the guesthouse stand on a 25-acre site, which visitors are free to enjoy. Ruth, by the way, is sister to Ethel Green Banta of Hope Farm, and she has some engaging childhood photos.

The Governor Holmes House
207 South Wall Street
Natchez, MS 39120
1-888-442-0166 or 601-442-2366
Fax: 601-442-0166
(Also available through Natchez Pilgrimage Tours)

Four suites with private baths in 1794 National Historic Landmark. Period furnishings. TV, phone available. Tour included. Full breakfast. Children over 14 only, smoking restricted, no pets. Credit card required for reservation. Seven-day cancellation policy. Innkeeper Robert Pully. Rates $105, extra person $30. Senior discount. AX, DS, MC, V. Pays commission to travel agents.

A 1794 date makes the two-story brick Governor Holmes House one of the oldest in Natchez. It was the residence of Gov. David Holmes both when he was territorial governor and when he became the first Mississippi governor upon the state's admission to the Union in December 1817. According to Robert Pully, owner/manager, it is one of the buildings in John James Audubon's painting of Natchez and may have once belonged to Jefferson Davis. Today it is filled with antique canopied beds, Oriental carpets, and period paintings.

Pully has had 30 years' experience at the Algonquin Hotel in New York, making him uniquely qualified to pamper guests, which he does. Our suite consisted of a small sitting room, bedroom, and bath. Hand-hewn support timbers, complete with adz marks, were visible in the brick outer and plaster inner walls. The unit opened onto a balcony furnished with wooden rocking chairs, and grape-loaded vines clung to the railing. The balcony looked out over a cozy brick-paved courtyard with a magnificent magnolia tree a full story taller than the two-story house. Antiques and tasteful decorative touches were everywhere; a large glass-fronted cabinet, which covered one wall of our bathroom, was filled with Oriental porcelain, and more pieces adorned the mantel in the sitting room.

Bob's full breakfast varies when guests stay more than one night. One offering is French toast with honey-mandarin sauce, and another is called pig-in-a-poke, a sort of Yorkshire pudding with bacon and hot maple syrup. Pully also serves an apple, egg, bacon casserole, and chopped ham and gravy over English muffins. Fruit, muffins, juice, and coffee or tea round out breakfast, and for other meals, he will make restaurant recommendations and reservations.

The Guest House Historic Inn
201 North Pearl Street
Natchez, MS 39120
601-442-1054
Fax: 601-442-1374

Seventeen rooms with private baths in 1840 National Register property. Antique and reproduction furnishings. TV, phone. Coffeemakers, antique shop next door. Continental breakfast. Corporate retreats, small meetings, and private parties. Children welcome, no smoking, small pets only. Reservation deposit with credit card required. Innkeepers Shawyn Mars and Thom Miller. Rates $94-$114, extra person $15. Senior discount except during pilgrimage. AX, DS; MC, V. Pays commission to travel agents.

With 17 rooms, the Guest House Historic Inn is the largest inn under one roof in Natchez. The massive Greek Revival building of red brick has four huge two-story Ionic columns across the front, and two graceful side galleries are supported by 16 smaller matching pillars.

The rooms contain double, queen, or king beds and are elegantly appointed in antiques and reproductions. Present owners Shawyn Mars and Thom Miller have operated the property since 1995, according to longtime manager Betty Williams.

Breakfast—a continental meal of fresh fruit, muffins, rolls, cereal, juice, milk, and coffee—is served in a sleek modern room that is also open to the public as a coffeehouse from 10 to 3 daily. Cappuccino is available during these hours, but no food.

Harper House
201 Arlington Avenue
Natchez, MS 39120
1-800-571-8848 or 601-445-5557

Harper House

Two units with private baths in 1890 Victorian home. Antique oak furnishings, Victorian decor. TV, phone available. Private entrance and parking. Full Southern breakfast. Children over 10 only, no smoking, no pets. Innkeeper Kay Warren. Rates $90-$170. MC, V. Pays commission to travel agents.

Set among large crepe myrtles in the Arlington Heights section of Natchez, Harper House is full of Victorian trim and charm. It was built near the end of the 19th century by Mary Florence Harper, of the Harpers Ferry, West Virginia, Harpers, and it remained in her family until 1974. Slender turned columns and a wooden railing adorn a front porch that leads partway around the two-story residence, and shutters and a transom frame double entry doors.

Most of the furniture is antique oak, and owners Kay and John Warren offer a three-bedroom suite with one bath upstairs and a bedroom with private bath on the first floor. The Warrens have been here since 1988, and Kay's artistic talents are displayed in her hand stenciling and stained-glass painting throughout the house.

Ordinarily, guests get a full Southern breakfast, but if they stay more than one night, Kay sometimes serves a continental the second morning. She points out that Harper House is within walking distance of much of historic downtown Natchez.

Highpoint

Highpoint
215 Linton Avenue
Natchez, MS 39120
1-800-283-4099 or 601-442-6963

Three rooms with private baths in 1890 Victorian home in Clifton Heights. Antique and period furnishings. TV in den, phone available. Varied full plantation breakfast. Complimentary evening beverages, snacks. Children over 12 only, designated smoking areas, no pets. Reservation required. Innkeepers Frank Bauer and John N. Davis. Rates $80-$100. Senior discount. MC, V. Pays commission to travel agents.

Built on the grounds of the old Clifton Plantation home, Highpoint is the oldest home in the first planned subdivision developed outside Natchez. The original plantation house was the only major Natchez mansion destroyed during the Civil War by Union troops, according to co-owner Frank Bauer. The Yankees razed it to make way for battlements in anticipation of a Rebel attack that never happened. The house was named Highpoint by Captain Prince, an early owner who operated the two steamboat ferries between Natchez and Vidalia.

Previously remodeled in the 1920s and in the 1950s, the home again underwent renovations in 1992. An original tub in one of the bathrooms sits on a bronze base, has no faucets, and pre-dates the claw-foot model. The Palladian window in the parlor is a reproduction of the original, which was found during restoration but could not be saved. The gardens and grounds are being revived to save and enhance some older Southern varieties of roses and other plants—even a relatively rare green rose. Highpoint was named 1997 Property of the Year by the Natchez Convention and Visitor Bureau.

Bauer also says that he will serve you a complimentary evening glass of wine, or a mint julep in his grandfather's silver julep cup, along with the snack du jour.

Hope Farm
147 Homochitto Street
Natchez, MS 39120
601-445-4848
(Also available through Natchez Pilgrimage Tours)

Four rooms with private baths in wing of 1775 National Register Creole Spanish-style mansion. Original antique furnishings. Tour included. Full Southern breakfast. No small children during pilgrimage, smoking on porches, no pets. Reservation deposit required. Innkeeper Ethel Green Banta. Rates $100, extra person $30. No credit cards.

Spanish governor Carlos de Grand-Pre was actually a Frenchman who found the Creole house at Hope Farm to his liking. One of the oldest residences in Natchez, the original building dates from 1775, and in 1789 the governor added an ell wing, forming a Spanish courtyard at the back. Set on a small rise at the corner of Duncan Avenue and Homochitto Street, the house features square columns supporting a sloping end-gabled

Hope Farm
Illustration by Rubia Sherry

roof, which extends to cover a front gallery that runs the length of the one-and-a-half-story structure.

The tree-shaded yard is planted in old-fashioned garden style with bulbs, azaleas, and small shrubs. Inside, cypress beams, low ceilings, and rare original Natchez antiques attest to the age of the home. The four guestrooms are located in the wing, and visitors who have stayed here include Gen. Douglas MacArthur, Lady Bird Johnson, and Eudora Welty.

Staffer Elizabeth Scaife, in the years that she has worked at Hope Farm, has served her full Southern breakfast to many prominent guests. The menu often features a sausage soufflé whose recipe is secret, but ham, bacon, biscuits, eggs, grits, homemade jellies, juice, and coffee are also served.

Linden
1 Linden Place
Natchez, MS 39120
1-800-254-6336 or 601-445-5472
Fax: 601-442-7548
Web site: www.natchezms.com/linden

Located just off Melrose Avenue. Seven rooms with private baths in 1792 National Register home. Federal antique furnishings. TV, phone available. Tour included. Full breakfast. Children over 10 only, smoking on galleries, no pets. Innkeeper Jeanette Feltus. Rates $90-$120, extra person $30. No credit cards. Pays commission to travel agents.

Linden

The earliest part of Linden was built by James Moore in 1792 on a Spanish Land Grant originally acquired by Sara Truly in 1785. Thomas B. Reed, first senator elected from Mississippi, bought it in 1818 and called it Reedland. In 1829 the senator sold the property to Dr. John Ker, who renamed it Linden. Through the years additions were made to both land and house, and in 1849, the estate was bought by Jane Gustine Conner and has been in her family ever since.

There may even be a ghost. Present owner Jeanette Feltus tells the story of a family member who lived at the house for a long time. As is common with many older people, he sometimes had trouble sleeping at night and would get up and walk around the house with his cane. He died in October a few years back, and on his birthday the following April 2, there were guests at Linden. The next morning three of them asked Mrs. Feltus who was tapping around with a cane during the night.

"Oh, that was Dick," she said.

"Well, where is he?"

"In heaven."

Mrs. Feltus adds that Linden's front door was copied for use in *Gone with the Wind,* and inside she has a fine collection of Hepplewhite, Chippendale, and Sheraton furniture. There are three guestrooms on the first floor, two on the second, and two in a wing, all of which open onto galleries. After morning coffee, guests take the full breakfast of ham, eggs, grits, biscuits, orange juice, and coffee or tea in the dining room or on the gallery, weather permitting.

Lisle House
205 State Street
Mailing Address: 701 North Union Street
Natchez, MS 39120
601-442-7680
Fax: 601-446-8260
(Also available through Natchez Pilgrimage Tours)

Two bedrooms with one bath in small 1880 cottage across from pilgrimage headquarters, rented as unit. Period furnishings. TV, phone. Self-catered expanded continental breakfast, stocked refrigerator. Call *about children, smoking outside, no pets. Reservation deposit required. Innkeeper Marie Perkins. Rates $125, extra person $35. AX. Pays commission to travel agents.*

Victorian Lisle House, only a block from the river, is convenient to everything downtown, with a restaurant next door on one side and The Corner lounge on the other. Natchez Pilgrimage Tours is directly across the street and usually handles reservations. Marie Perkins and her husband own Shields Town House, also listed in this guide.

The small, cozy cottage, always rented as a unit, contains two bedrooms with tester beds, a parlor, kitchen, and dining room, making it ideal for a family with children over 12 or two couples traveling together. The kitchen provides a convenient place for guests to prepare their own meals, and the refrigerator is stocked for breakfast.

Mark Twain Guest House
25 Silver Street
P.O. Box 0
Natchez, MS 39121
601-446-8023

Three rooms with shared bath in 1830 two-story brick building in Natchez-Under-the-Hill. Some period furnishings, family pieces. Phone downstairs, washer/dryer available. On-street parking. Continental breakfast. Saloon downstairs. Children welcome, smoking okay, no pets. Innkeeper Andre Farish. Rates $55-$75. AX, MC, V. Travel agent's commission may be added.

The Mark Twain Guest House is in another part of Natchez. Under-the-Hill was once a rowdy, brawling riverfront where gamblers, boatmen, and prostitutes sought business and pleasure. It was the port area where the steamboats loaded and unloaded goods during the day and where their crews partied at night. Some of this flavor is maintained today.

To register at the Mark Twain, you must go into the saloon, above which the units are located. Owner Andre Farish points out that the inn has had a checkered career as brothel, pool hall, and bakery. Today, the comfortable guestrooms feature fireplaces and a balcony with one of the best river views in

Natchez. The continental breakfast here includes pastries, juice, and coffee.

Farish also operates the Under-the-Hill Saloon and says that they have live entertainment on weekends from March through December and crawfish boils in season. For meals at other times try the nearby Magnolia Grill, which features good gumbo, catfish, and sandwiches, or the Riverboat Casino, which is within easy walking distance.

Mary Magnolia's Bed & Breakfast
501 Madison Street
Natchez, MS 39120
601-442-4161
Fax: 601-445-8895
E-mail: marymag1@aol.com

Two rooms with two baths in restored two-story 1860 home. Antique furnishings. TV, VCR, phone, intercom, whirlpool, robes. Cafe au lait and beignets on balcony at 8, full Southern breakfast at 8:30. No children, smoking on balcony, no pets. Credit card required for reservation. Innkeeper Mary Ann Henderson. Rates $90-$120. Senior discount. MC, V. Pays commission to travel agents.

Mary Ann Henderson informed us that she is the first African-American in Mississippi to become an innkeeper, and she left a prestigious Hollywood job with ABC to do it. As she says, "I'm proof that you can come home again."

Her antebellum inn in the Historic District had been mostly

*Mary Magnolia's
Bed & Breakfast*

restored when she bought it. Antique furnishings grace the two bedrooms, and in addition to TVs and phones, there is music in every room, along with an intercom. Her flower-filled patio is also home to doves and pigeons that flutter across the enclosed space when a guest steps outside.

Mary stresses that her main interest is innkeeping, even though she takes part in various civic activities. She is sticking to two rooms for awhile because that is what she can comfortably handle without help. Her breakfast is really two. Guests get cafe au lait and beignets on the upstairs gallery at 8, then come down to the dining room for the full Southern fare at 8:30. This may be eggs, sausage, and grits with all the traditional Southern accompaniments or maybe French toast on the second morning.

Mary still does some TV work, but she said in an interview with Mark LaFrancis in the *Natchez Democrat,* "You know, all the while I worked in the film and television business, I kept feeling the tug of Natchez . . . it is heartwarming to have so many people welcome me back to Natchez and offer to help out with my business enterprises."

Miss Lucy's Cottage
707 State Street
Natchez, MS 39120
601-445-8685
(Also available through Natchez Pilgrimage Tours)

One bedroom with bath in 1850 two-story red brick cottage with white stucco front and black shutters. Some antique furnishings. TV, phone. Self-catered breakfast, stocked refrigerator. Complimentary beverages. No children, smoking outside, no pets. Reservation deposit $50. Innkeeper Bernard Wood. Rates $125. No credit cards. Pays commission to travel agents.

This elegant little property delights the eye when the guest takes in its petite proportions and understated style. The single-gabled two-story red brick cottage, which probably dates to the same circa-1850 period as the house behind which it stands, provides very private accommodations for two. Downstairs, a sitting room gives onto a kitchen where guests may use a stocked refrigerator to prepare a breakfast to their own tastes.

The upstairs suite has a comfortably furnished bedroom,

bath, and another sitting area. A small balcony, where there is ample room for two to enjoy a sundowner, overlooks a colorful brick-pathed formal garden. Miss Lucy's Cottage seems the perfect spot for the couple desiring a weekend away from it all, and as owner Bernard Wood points out, "it is within walking distance of everything."

Monmouth Plantation
36 Melrose Avenue
Natchez, MS 39120
1-800-828-4531 or 601-442-5852
Fax: 601-446-7762

Located at the junction of Quitman Parkway and Melrose Avenue. Nineteen rooms with private baths in 1818 National Historic Landmark Greek Revival mansion, carriage house, garden cottages, and old kitchen. Original antique furnishings. TV, phone, robes, nightly turndown with chocolates. Tour included. Full Southern breakfast, fresh flowers in dining room. Dinner by reservation. Honor bar. Children over 14 only, no smoking, no pets. Reservation deposit required. Seven-day cancellation policy. Innkeepers Mr. and Mrs. Ronald Riches. Rates $140-$370, extra person $37. AX, DS, MC, V. Pays commission to travel agents.

Monmouth was built in 1818 by Natchez postmaster John Hankinson, but he did not get to enjoy it long. He and his wife both died of yellow fever that same year. In 1826, it became the plantation home of John A. Quitman, later to be a Mexican War hero, general, congressman, and governor. He was appointed

Monmouth Plantation

military governor of Mexico City for his bravery. He died at Monmouth in 1858, apparently of food poisoning contracted in Washington, D.C., at a banquet for Pres. James Buchanan.

With four huge square columns supporting the front balcony, the mansion is a magnificent sight. Inside, antiques original to the Quitman family grace the rooms. Guests have the use of the Quitman study downstairs and a sitting room upstairs. Overnight accommodations include seven rooms in the main house, four in the carriage house, four in two garden cottages, and four in the old kitchen. A stroll around the 24 acres of landscaped grounds reveals gazebos, a pond with ducks and bridge, and an old cemetery.

In addition to the full Southern breakfast, a five-course candlelight dinner is available in the formal dining room by reservation for $37 per person exclusive of drinks, gratuity, and tax. After soup, salad, and sorbet, the entree might be grilled shrimp with mustard sauce, filet mignon with béarnaise, or grilled swordfish with herb butter. The meal is served nightly with a changing menu every night, and there are always two entrees to choose from, followed by dessert and coffee.

Oakland Plantation
1124 Lower Woodville Road
Natchez, MS 39120
1-800-824-0355 or 601-445-5101
Fax: 601-442-5182
E-mail: maxskimr@bkbank.com

Oakland Plantation

Located about nine miles south of Natchez off Highway 61. Three rooms with private baths in 1785 two-story Colonial brick guesthouse. Antique furnishings. TV in dining area, phone available. Kitchen, barbecue grill, tennis court, nature trails, fishing ponds. Tour included. Full Southern breakfast. Children welcome, smoking on porches only, no pets. Reservation deposit required. Innkeeper Andrew Peabody. Rates $80-$140. AX, MC, V. Pays commission to travel agents.

The original house at Oakland Plantation—the one where guests stay today—was built about 1785 and is believed to be the oldest brick house in the Natchez area, according to owner Andrew Peabody. A church building on the grounds behind was constructed earlier. The main mansion dates from 1821, he says, and additions were made in 1831.

Among the early guests at Oakland were Andrew Jackson and Rachel Robards. Rachel stayed about five months while Jackson was in Nashville, then he came back down and courted her at Oakland. They were married in August 1791 at Springfield Plantation, home of Judge Thomas Green, the father of Oakland's owner, Abner. Unfortunately, in 1793, the couple learned that Rachel's divorce from previous husband Lewis Robards had not been final at the time of their wedding. They were married again in Nashville in January 1794.

Oakland remained in the Green family until after the Civil War, and in 1880 it was bought by a former slave, Alex Mazique. His family maintained ownership until 1956, when Peabody bought it.

The main house and the guesthouse contain some of the oldest furniture that we have seen. A circa-1520 wooden sea-captain's chest with sturdy iron hardware is decorated with carved figures of Native Americans outfitted in headdresses and other accoutrements of the period. This, according to Peabody, helps to date it, since it is only 28 years after Christopher Columbus first landed in the New World. Several other 17th- and 18th-century pieces are scattered throughout the two houses.

Visitors can truly appreciate the grandeur of secluded Oakland when they step onto the magnificent 110-foot-long front porch. The owner also points out that the home was built in two stages, with the original rooms having wooden walls, while the newer parts are plastered.

Today, the 360-acre plantation is a game preserve and has eight ponds, four of which are good for fishing. Andrew says nature trails abound, and a court used by his tennis-pro wife is also available for guests. He adds that breakfast is Southern—grits, bacon, eggs, and biscuits. To reach the plantation, drive 8.7 miles south from the Jefferson Davis Hospital on Highway 61, turn right at the Oakland sign, and follow additional signs.

Ravenna
8 Ravenna Lane
Natchez, MS 39120
601-445-8516
Fax: 601-445-0052
(Also available through Natchez Pilgrimage Tours)

Two rooms with private baths in 1835 National Register property. Antique furnishings. TV, phone available, swimming pool, fireplace. Tour included. Full Southern breakfast. Children welcome, smoking on porches, no pets. One-night reservation deposit required. Innkeeper Catherine Brandon Morgan. Rates $95-$110. No credit cards. Pays commission to travel agents.

Wealthy cotton broker William Harris and his wife, Caroline Harrison Harris, built Ravenna in 1835. Her uncle, William Henry Harrison, later became U.S. president. The fine old double-galleried, double-columned mansion has an outstanding three-story elliptical stairway and is also noted for its elegant woodwork.

The two guestrooms, one above the other, are nearly identical, with massive beds and other antique furnishings. Owner

Ravenna

Catherine Brandon Morgan says her guests seem to enjoy Ravenna, which is located in the Historic District, surrounded by three acres of old informal gardens, and within walking distance of downtown, the river, and many other historical sites. Overnight guests also receive a private tour of the home.

Riverside Bed & Breakfast
211 Clifton Avenue
Natchez, MS 39120
601-446-5730

Three rooms with private baths in restored two-story 1858 National Register home overlooking Mississippi River. Period furnishings. Cable TV, some phones. Full plantation breakfast. No children, smoking in designated areas, no pets. Reservation deposit required. Seven-day cancellation policy; cancellation fee charged. Innkeeper Durell Epperson. Rates $85-$150. No credit cards, but takes personal checks, traveler's checks, cash. Pays commission to travel agents.

Durell Epperson started out in Corinth, Mississippi, and somehow, from Corinth, found his way to New Orleans, where he stayed for nearly 30 years. He came to Natchez, and Riverside, in 1988 and says that this is where he intends to remain. With his easy, friendly, outgoing manner, he manages to tell some good stories and drop several one-liners on you before you even get in the house. However, one thing he is secretive about is breakfasts, but he declares that they are full Southern plantation—he only shares the menus with his guests.

In 1999, Riverside was somewhat difficult to reach. Work was ongoing toward stabilizing the bluff on which the home and a number of others perch. Epperson says that Riverside, built in 1858 as the overseer's house for Clifton Plantation, was the only house on this bluff not destroyed during the Civil War. He states that it did not become a two-story house until the second floor was added in 1903.

Today, Riverside has been brought to a level of elegance that it probably never knew before. A common room across the entire front of the second floor gives a sweeping, and possibly unexcelled, view of the river. Guestrooms are elegantly appointed, and one contains a unique iron tester bed, crown topped to indicate that it was built for Spanish royalty, Epperson notes.

Shields Town House

Shields Town House
701 North Union Street
Natchez, MS 39120
601-442-7680
Fax: 601-446-8260
(Also available through Natchez Pilgrimage Tours)

Two one-bedroom suites with private baths in original dependencies on grounds of 1858 National Register Greek Revival home. Period furnishings. TV, phone. Full kitchen, lighted garage parking. Continental breakfast. Call about children, smoking outside, no pets. Innkeepers Marie and W. S. Perkins. Rates $120, extra person $35. No credit cards, but takes personal checks, traveler's checks, cash. Pays commission to travel agents.

Begun in 1858 and finished in 1860, Shields Town House was the last house of its kind completed in Natchez before the Civil War, according to current owner W. S. Perkins. The one-and-a-half-story Greek Revival structure was first home to Maurice and Isabelle Stockman Lisle. He owned Natchez Foundry, and she was the daughter of local mayor John Stockman.

The Lisles sold the residence to Wilmer Shields in 1869, and it became the Shields Town House. The Perkinses acquired the home in 1978 after it had been vacant for several years and restored it with the help of their architect son.

Fluted Doric columns frame a paneled entrance door with transom and sidelights. Inside, elegant marble mantels are found in the parlor, the dining room, and a bedroom. Among the many 18th- and 19th-century antique furnishings, there is a dresser that came from the Tennessee home of 11th U.S. president James K. Polk.

An ell-shaped building—once Shields' office—plus the original kitchen now provide overnight accommodations for guests. Each suite has a bedroom, sitting room, bath, private courtyard, and kitchen stocked for continental breakfast—melon and other fruit, homemade orange-pecan muffins, fresh croissants, and raspberry jam, juice, coffee, and tea. A refrigerator and stove make it possible for guests to prepare other meals if they desire.

T.A.S.S. House Bed & Breakfast
404 South Commerce Street
Natchez, MS 39120
601-445-4663
Fax: 601-445-5161
E-mail: tasshse@telepak.net

Four rooms with private baths in circa-1893 National Register property in Historic Garden District. Period furnishings. TV in two rooms, phone available, working fireplaces. Doors open into hall with microwave, refrigerator, iron, ironing board. Full Southern breakfast. Other meals by request—honeymoons, anniversaries, opera-goers. No preteens, no smoking, no pets. One-night reservation deposit required or credit card number. Innkeepers Marilyn and Robert Costa. Rates $105-$210, extra person $10. AX, MC, V.

T.A.S.S. House Bed & Breakfast

Robert and Marilyn Costa call their double-columned, double-galleried Greek Revival home T.A.S.S. House "Gay Nineties" Bed & Breakfast. Marilyn says the "T.A.S.S." originally stood for Tea, Antiques, Sherry, and Sass. They now like for it to mean Tea, Antiques, and Southern Sass. The circa-1893 house is loaded with period furnishings. In fact, Robert says he probably has more than anyone in Natchez. This statement could very well be true since he and Marilyn also have an antique shop three blocks away at Commerce and Main streets.

Rooms here have colorful names—Ivory, Aqua, Red, and Blue—denoting, of course, their color schemes. The Blue and Red rooms are usually combined and rented as a suite, since they share a bath. The Blue room is especially notable for its very Victorian Eastlake furnishings. All of the rooms have working fireplaces.

Breakfast at T.A.S.S. House is pretty much what the guest desires, says Marilyn. She states that baked French toast is a popular item, and, in addition to the regular breakfast menu, they sometimes serve mimosas, particularly for notable events. When guests are out late, as in opera season, breakfast evolves into brunch to accommodate the late risers. Marilyn will also prepare other meals by reservation.

Texada Tavern
222 South Wall Street
Natchez, MS 39120
601-445-4283
(Also available through Natchez Pilgrimage Tours)

Four bedrooms with private baths in 1792 three-story National Register home plus two-bedroom guesthouse accommodating four. Elegant antique furnishings. TV in central upstairs sitting room, phone available. Full breakfast. Children restricted, no smoking, no pets. Reservation deposit required. Innkeeper Margaret Moss. Rates $100, extra person $25. No credit cards. Pays commission to travel agents.

Michael Solibellas obtained a Spanish Land Grant for the Texada Tavern property in 1792 and probably began construction of the house that same year. But the man for whom it is named, Don Manuel Garcia de Texada, acquired it in 1798 and

Texada Tavern
Illustration by Rubia Sherry

apparently enlarged it. The Spanish-born Texada rented at least a portion of the house out, and an early tenant was Beaumont's Hotel and City Tavern. In 1806, John Callender was operating the American Eagle Tavern in the same location.

When Texada died in 1817, the year that Mississippi entered the Union, Edward Turner bought the property. A prominent citizen and politician, he served as Natchez mayor, state attorney general, speaker of the state house of representatives, and chief justice of the Mississippi Supreme Court. During Turner's occupancy, the state legislature sometimes assembled here.

Texada Tavern has been meticulously restored by present owners Dr. George and Margaret Moss. As they point out, it was the first brick house in Natchez and probably second in age only to King's Tavern, built in 1789. The Mosses have furnished their home with American and European antiques and covered the floors with Persian rugs, one of which dates to the 1790s.

They have a lady's folding fan bought in England in 1775 for the wedding of one of George's great-great-great-great-grandmothers. It has become a family custom for the girls to use it in their weddings as "something old."

Since 1991, the Mosses have provided complimentary accommodations for opera cast members to help promote a May season in Natchez. They also said that their travels nowadays are primarily to see their grandchildren participate in athletics; they have 12.

The Victorian
610 North Pearl Street
Natchez, MS 39120
601-442-3510
Web site: www.bcity.com/thevictorian

Five rooms with four baths in circa-1900 Queen Anne Victorian home. Period furnishings. Cable TV, phone. Full buffet breakfast. Honeymoon and golf packages. Children over 12 only, smoking on porch and patio, no pets. Reservation deposit one-half night's stay. Innkeepers Ronnie Bridges and John Duchkar. Rates $69-$160. MC, V. Pays commission to travel agents.

The Victorian is a mirror image of the house on its right. The two were built by brothers around 1900, and the other remains in the hands of the original family. A veranda curves gracefully around the Victorian's front and is loaded with flowers and greenery. The yard also brims with roses, camellias, azaleas, and other flowering plants.

Inside, the common rooms are furnished with antiques, and innkeeper Ronnie Bridges proudly notes that many of them came from his grandmother. A sunroom along one side of the house displays the largest collection of cookie jars that we have ever seen. But when we asked about a pottery train (engine, coal car, and two coaches), we learned that they were all whiskey decanters.

The bedrooms are comfortably furnished with contemporary king and queen beds. Breakfast is ample and tends to run toward a variety of casseroles rather than typical grits and eggs.

Wensel House
206 Washington Street
Natchez, MS 39120
1-888-775-8577 or 601-445-8577
Fax: 601-442-2525
(Also available through Natchez Pilgrimage Tours)

Three rooms with double and single beds and private baths in National Register 1888 restored Victorian townhouse plus two-bedroom, one-bath suite in cottage. Period furnishings. TV, VCR, phone.

Wensel House
Illustration by Ron Miller

Hairdryer, ironing board, iron available. Full Southern breakfast at 8 in dining room. Complimentary beverages and fruit. Call about children, smoking on porches, no pets. Innkeepers Ron and Mimi Miller. Rates $85-$100, extra person $15. MC, V. Pays commission to travel agents.

This two-story 1888 Victorian townhouse was built by Theodore Wensel, who was reared at Rosalie, the large 1820 brick mansion near the site of old Fort Rosalie. According to prior manager Jean Moffett, there is no ghost in the house, but there is one out back. Some nights a Kentucky colonel-type gentleman with white hair and beard and a white linen suit escorts people from one house to the next. Present innkeeper Ron Miller says that he has never seen the ghost, but if Jean says he is there, he is.

Wensel House's guest bedrooms are all upstairs and furnished with antique and family pieces, and the cottage also contains family pieces. Coffee is ready at 7 A.M. An early continental breakfast is available on the sideboard in the formal dining room, and full breakfast is served family style for all guests at 8 on weekdays and 8:30 on weekends. The meal consists of biscuits, eggs, bacon, ham, jelly, fruit, juice, milk, coffee, and tea.

Weymouth Hall
Illustration by Rubia Sherry

Weymouth Hall
1 Cemetery Road
P.O. Box 1091
Natchez, MS 39121
601-445-2304
(Also available through Natchez Pilgrimage Tours)

Five rooms with private baths in 1855 Greek Revival National Register mansion overlooking the river and City Cemetery. Antique and reproduction furnishings. TV, phone, fax machine available. Full Southern breakfast. Weddings, receptions, and corporate meetings. Children over 14 only, no smoking, no pets. Reservation deposit required. Innkeepers Troyce and Lynda Guice. Rates $95-$105, extra person $35. MC, V. Pays commission to travel agents.

Located on a bluff overlooking the Mississippi River, Weymouth Hall offers a panoramic view of the area and breathtaking sunsets. Built in 1855 by Judge Ruben Bullock, the Greek Revival home survived occupation by Federal troops during the Civil War. Erosion of the loess hill on which Weymouth stands for a time presented the danger that it would tumble into the river, but the prior owners stabilized the ground by hauling in thousands of yards of earth, shoring up and preserving the fine old mansion.

All Weymouth guest accommodations are in the main house, which is filled with antique and reproduction furniture. The ambience of the formal dining room enhances the complete breakfast of ham, sausage, eggs, grits, blueberry muffins, juice, and coffee. Recessed porches offer relaxing spots to sit and enjoy the scenery in late afternoon.

Just across Cemetery Road, the Natchez City Cemetery was once a cotton field for the house, according to former owner Gene Weber. That was a long time ago, though, because the burial ground is one of the oldest in Mississippi and the last resting place of most of the town's prominent early residents.

OCEAN SPRINGS

Ocean Springs got its name when a doctor established a sanatorium here in 1854; the local spring waters had medicinal properties, according to the Native Americans in the area. This part of Mississippi was settled much earlier, however, with the first permanent European settlement taking place in 1699. Today, the town is a resort area and artist colony, and some places to visit include the Walter Anderson Museum of Art, Shearwater Pottery, The Doll House, Gulf Islands National Seashore, Sandhill Crane National Wildlife Refuge, and Fort Maurepas, built by the French in 1699 while Ocean Springs was still part of colonial Louisiana.

One of the best activities is a stroll down the streets of the well-preserved old town. Restaurants, shops, and galleries vie for your attention. Among the good places to eat are Martha's Tea Room and Salvetti Brothers Italian Restaurant. We had lunch at both places—chicken and seafood salads at Martha's and a baked eggplant parmigiana sandwich at Salvetti's. We drank Barq's root beer at both. Other restaurants include Germaine's, which was formerly Trilby's, and Jocelyn's, with the former chef from Trilby's.

Festivals in Ocean Springs include the Elks Mardi Gras Parade and Fort Maurepas Living History Weekend in January, Ocean Springs Pilgrimage in March, Re-enactment of the Landing of D'Iberville in 1699 in April, Art Walk in August, Great Oaks Storytelling Festival in October, and Peter Anderson Arts and

Crafts Festival in November. For additional information, contact the Ocean Springs Chamber of Commerce, P.O. Box 187, Ocean Springs, MS 39564, 228-875-4424.

The Acorn
3305 Government Street
Ocean Springs, MS 39564
228-875-4963
Fax: 228-872-0571

1909 1,000-square-foot cottage with bedroom; bath; two closets; full kitchen with refrigerator/freezer, electric stove and oven, microwave; separate dining room; living room; and three porches, on two acres of land. Some antique furnishings. Cable TV, VCR, stereo with CD player, phone, answering machine, computer, washer/dryer, gas grill. Coupon for continental breakfast at Bayview Gourmet. Children welcome, no smoking, no pets. Innkeepers Lana and Steve Robinson. Rates $50-$65, weekly and monthly rates available. Pays commission to travel agents.

Innkeepers Lana and Steve Robinson's daughter, Sandra, met us at this B&B, told us her parents were on vacation, and showed us through the charming cottage. She was able to answer most of our questions, but for the ones she could not answer, she took us across the yard to Lana's home and called Lana so that we could interview her over the phone. Sandra did tell us an interesting story of how her parents had bought the matching Art Deco safe and sideboard for the cottage dining

The Acorn

room—at different times and different places. They purchased one in Mobile, Alabama, and the other on the Mississippi coast. The bedroom is also tastefully furnished in pieces from the early 20th century.

The living room, with garden windows that overlook colorful azaleas and camellias in season, has a queen-size sofa sleeper and a daybed. Including the bedroom the cottage sleeps up to five. Double French doors from the dining room lead to a small private sun porch, and a 12-foot-deep back porch provides rocking chairs and a swing. The third porch is screened, can be accessed from either the living room or the bedroom, and is a nice spot to enjoy a morning cup of coffee with a freshly baked muffin. Coupons from Bayview Gourmet restaurant are provided for continental breakfasts.

Cottage Retreat
507 East Beach
Ocean Springs, MS 39564
228-875-7049

Two-bedroom 1940s cottage with bath near beach behind 1890 home designed by Louis Sullivan and Frank Lloyd Wright. Eclectic contemporary furnishings. Cable TV, phone, canoe and bikes available. No breakfast. Children welcome, no smoking, no pets. Reservation deposit required. Innkeepers Tom and Peggy Butera. Rates $180 for two persons for two-night weekend, weekly and monthly rates available. No credit cards.

Of her cottage, Peggy Butera says, self-deprecatingly, "It is not impressive, and it definitely is not furnished with my grandmother's antiques," and she quickly adds, "but it's comfortable, and people have a good time here." She also says, "But I don't do breakfast, so I guess that makes it a guesthouse and not a B&B."

What is impressive is the history of her house. The octagonally designed home was one of three houses that Louis Sullivan had built along this stretch of the coast when Frank Lloyd Wright was his pupil. The interior is typical for the pair, with built-in window seats and curly pine floors, walls, and ceilings. The house was expanded twice in the 1950s and 1960s, straight back, and with an additional identical octagon at the back. Even though there are no accommodations in the main house, Peggy is happy for guests to come in for a visit.

The cottage itself was built in the 1940s during the World War II Keesler Air Force Base population influx and provides two bedrooms, a bath, and a screened front porch. With woods behind it, a beach in front, and Gulf Islands National Seashore, the harbor, and Shearwater Pottery nearby, it is an ideal retreat for nature lovers, and the Buteras furnish a canoe and bikes. Peggy is employed part time at the pottery, and husband Tom is in the medical products business and maintains his office at home. Even though Peggy does not provide breakfast, she does recommend restaurants, and some of her favorites are Salvetti's, Germaine's Lagniappe, Jocelyn's, and Phoenician Gardens.

Dogwood Place
1312 Porter Avenue
Ocean Springs, MS 39564
228-875-4468

One suite with private bath in 1914 Gulf Coast Cottage-style home. Family antique furnishings. Two TVs, two phones, robes, kitchen access, two bicycles available. Continental breakfast. No children, smoking outside, accommodations for pets on request. Innkeepers Donnalee and Sonny Dick. Rates $65. Senior discount. No credit cards, but takes personal checks.

We were amazed at the surprisingly spacious interior of Dogwood Place. With a center hall running the length of the

Dogwood Place

house, and rows of rooms on either side, it gives Donnalee Dick ample room to provide a suite for guests. The comfortably furnished guest quarters include TVs in both bedroom and parlor, as well as a phone in each.

Visitors also have use of the large hall parlor with books available for reading, and an attractive back gallery with a swing and wicker furniture. The shaded yard is filled with plants and colorful blooming flowers. Donnalee says her breakfast usually includes her special Yogurt Parfait, and might be French toast or cereal.

Ruskin Carriage Inn
410 Ruskin Avenue
Ocean Springs, MS 39564
228-872-8161

One suite with bath, kitchenette, and private entrance across courtyard from main home. Contemporary furnishings, handicap accessible. TV, phone available. Continental breakfast. Call about children, no smoking, no pets. Innkeepers James and Joan Pylate. Rates $75. No credit cards, but takes personal checks. Pays commission to travel agents.

Innkeeper Joan Pylate said that her bed and breakfast quarters started as a storeroom, was considered for a game room complete with pool table, but ended up as a suite for guests. She describes herself as "a damn Yankee" from Chicago and husband James as a "Biloxi boy with a lot of good stories." Actually, she has been in Biloxi since the 1970s and has spent

Ruskin Carriage Inn

much of her time in real estate. The affable innkeeper, who had only been in the inn business about three months when we were there, said that it had been a delightful experience, especially since she enjoyed meeting new people and bed and breakfast people were always so nice.

Joan's guesthouse is entered from the courtyard, where guests may take breakfast if they wish. In addition to the bathroom and bedroom area with its queen-size bed and lots of pillows, there is also a kitchen with microwave, coffeemaker, and refrigerator containing fruit juice, cold drinks, and bottled water. The water became a staple when one guest suggested it to Joan. For breakfast she provides cereal, fresh fruit, bagels, coffee and tea, or a voucher good at a nearby French bakery.

Shadowlawn
112A Shearwater Drive
Ocean Springs, MS 39564
228-875-6945
Fax: 228-875-6595
E-mail: shadowos@datasync.com
Web site: www.gcww/shadowlawn/

Four rooms with private baths in 1907 National Register property built as a summer home. Antique furnishings. TV, phone available. Private beach. Full breakfast. Children over 14 only, no smoking, no pets. Credit card required for reservation. 72-hour cancellation policy. Innkeepers Bill and Nancy Wilson. Rates $100-$125. Senior discount. MC, V. Pays commission to travel agents.

Shadowlawn

Located on the shore of Mississippi Sound, Shadowlawn is the only house on the Mississippi Gulf Coast that does not have a road between it and the water, according to innkeeper Bill Wilson. Mr. and Mrs. John L. Dickey, grandparents of Bill's wife, Nancy, purchased the house in 1923 as a summer retreat from the humid heat of New Orleans. Traveling here by car, ferry, or train, they spent their summers enjoying the warm waters and cool breezes. The serene atmosphere has been maintained by Bill and Nancy, with guests invited to relax in the rockers and swings on the wide, screened, Gulf-facing porch or wander the grounds filled with majestic old oaks and dotted with small garden spots. Since the front lawn runs down to the water, they also have a private beach. Nancy has retained many of her family's pieces in furnishing and decorating the home.

The Wilsons are especially proud of their 30 x 30-foot water garden and their 150-bush rose bed. They give credit to their landscaper, who was head gardener in Düsseldorf, Germany for many years. They are also the proud owners of two Walter Anderson originals—a large painting called *David & Goliath* and a colorful vase that has been authenticated by the staff at Shearwater Pottery.

Breakfast here may be fruit, muffins, quiche, an egg dish, a meat, biscuits, and gravy, or some combination of these. They have furnished two of their specialty bread recipes.

Carrot-Pineapple Bread

2 eggs
1 cup sugar
$1/2$ tsp. salt
1 tsp. cinnamon
$1^1/2$ cups all-purpose flour
$2/3$ cup cooking oil
1 cup grated carrot
1 tsp. vanilla
1 tsp. baking powder
1 cup crushed pineapple, drained
1 tsp. baking soda

Beat eggs and sugar together. Add remaining ingredients

and beat well. Bake 25 minutes at 350 degrees. Makes 12 muffins or three small loaves.

Orange Breakfast Ring

³/₄ cup sugar
3 tbsp. grated orange peel
2 pkg. of 10, or 3 pkgs. of 6, buttermilk biscuits
¹/₃ cup melted butter
3-oz.-pkg. cream cheese
¹/₂ cup powdered sugar
2 tbsp. orange juice

Grease a Bundt pan. Combine sugar and orange peel. Dip biscuits in melted butter and roll in sugar and orange peel mixture. Place in pan and bake 20 minutes or until golden brown at 350 degrees. Combine cream cheese and powdered sugar. Add orange juice and beat. Drizzle over hot biscuits.

The Wilson House Inn
6312 Allen Road
Ocean Springs, MS 39565
1-800-872-6933 or 228-875-6933
Fax: 228-875-6933
E-mail: wilsonhouse@Digiscape.com

Six rooms with private baths in two-story 1923 log house. Antique furnishings. TV/VCR available, phone available, fireplaces in two

The Wilson House Inn

rooms. Full Southern breakfast. Call about other meals. Children over 10 only, smoking outside, no pets. Reservation deposit with credit card required. Innkeepers Delissa and Brian Britt. Rates $49-$79. 10 percent senior discount. AX, MC, V. Pays commission to travel agents.

It was pouring down rain when we arrived for our appointment at the Wilson House, and we sat in the car until it slacked up a bit, then grabbed our umbrellas and ran for the front porch of the log home. Innkeeper Delissa Britt met us at the door and, after inviting us in, immediately brought us a dry towel to blot ourselves. A delightful aroma was coming from the kitchen, and she said she was baking bread for a sick friend and offered us some. We reluctantly declined, since we had just eaten.

Delissa said that her two-story log home was built in 1922-23 by a realtor named Cox and was originally located north of Gulfport on Highway 49. It became the home of the Joel Pinson Wilson family, who planted acres of orange orchards as well as many other trees and flowers. The surrounding community became "Orange Grove" and the house was eventually acquired by the only son, Clarke B. Wilson, who was, himself, an excellent horticulturist.

The younger Wilson provided many azaleas and camellias to renowned Bellingrath Gardens near Mobile, Alabama. He also operated Wilson Farm Nurseries with his wife, Marjorie, until the 1980s. She was a journalist who wrote and illustrated a weekly gardening column, "Gardening Along the Coast," in Biloxi's Sun Herald newspaper for over 50 years.

The Britts moved the home to its present site in 1994, completely renovated it, added six bathrooms, removed, cleaned, and replaced the original brick in the fireplaces, and opened their bed and breakfast. Some furnishings are original to the house, and others are family pieces.

Delissa's full breakfasts may include biscuits, ham and eggs, pancakes, or other typical Southern fare.

OXFORD

Oxford is the home of "Ole Miss"—the University of Mississippi—and the birthplace of novelist William Faulkner.

The town was built in 1836 from land bought from a Chickasaw Indian woman, and the university began in 1844.

Our first stop in Oxford was for lunch at Smitty's Restaurant, just south of the square. This diner is a favorite breakfast spot and was once a hangout for Faulkner. We ate baked chicken, squash, string beans, mashed and sweet potatoes, and apple cobbler from the buffet. As we were eating, a lady, obviously part of the establishment, asked us if we were going to the ball-game. That explained the bumper-to-bumper traffic and hordes of people we had seen on the way into town. Ole Miss lost a basketball encounter with Kentucky that day.

This thriving, lively university town features a courthouse square surrounded by shops and restaurants, including a book-store and an art gallery. The latter was displaying sculptures by our newfound friend, Floyd Shaman, from Cleveland.

It took us awhile, but we finally located Rowan Oak, Faulkner's home for many years. Huge old cedar trees line the pathway to the two-story, columned Greek Revival home where the writer did much of his work. The room that he added and called "the office" contains his typewriter on a small desk, a sin-gle bed, an old pair of boots, and, on the wall, his notes for his Pulitzer Prize winning novel, *A Fable*, set during World War I. Upstairs, one bedroom displays a pair of shoes and a shoeshine box by a double bed with polish and brush out, as if the writer were about to give them a shine.

Barksdale-Isom House
1003 Jefferson Avenue
Oxford, MS 38655
1-800-236-5696 or 662-236-5600
Fax: 662-236-6763

Six rooms with private baths in two-story circa-1838 National Register house. Antique furnishings. TV, phone. Full Southern gourmet breakfast. Caters parties and receptions. Afternoon hors d'oeuvres and drinks. Children over 12 only, no smoking, no pets. Reservation required. 48-hour cancellation policy. Innkeeper Susan Barksdale. Rates $150-$175. AX, MC, V.

Barksdale-Isom House

Plush and elegant Barksdale-Isom House has been impeccably restored, expertly and authentically decorated, and furnished with 17th- and 18th-century antiques. To walk in the door is to enter the pages of 19th-century history. The original structure was built in 1835 by Dr. Thomas Isom and was the first apothecary in Lafayette County, called "Isom Place and Drug Store House."

Dr. Isom began with a three-room log cabin, which is still incorporated into the home. These three rooms are really two large rooms with a hall between them and were the basis for the rest of the structure. The year 1838 is thought to be the date of additional construction because the numbers were found scratched on a foundation stone. Before that, while it was still the apothecary, Dr. Isom met and married Sarah McGehee, who had come from Abbeville, South Carolina, to visit her twin sister.

As Isom became more prosperous, he added more to the house, so that it came to be an outstanding example of Greek Revival architecture. It was Isom who named Oxford after the university in England, hoping that the college here would reach that same height. In 1860 he tried to prevent Mississippi's secession from the Union but ended up signing the ordinance because he saw that was what the people wanted.

During the Civil War, Isom served as a surgeon, operating a

hospital in Virginia and then opening one on the University of Mississippi campus after the Battle of Shiloh. He treated more than 1,500 Union and Confederate wounded, and U. S. Grant was so appreciative of his efforts that he stationed two men at the house to prevent its destruction. The home is said to be the setting for William Faulkner's short story "A Rose for Emily," and when manager Scott Rea was showing us through, he pointed out the Rose Room.

Barksdale-Isom House furnished two of their breakfast recipes.

B & I Cheese Grits

2 cans chicken broth
1¹/₂ cans water
2 tsp. salt
2 cups uncooked grits
24 oz. shredded cheddar cheese
Tabasco
¹/₂ cup butter
4 eggs
1¹/₂ cups milk
4 bunches green onions, chopped
1 tsp. chopped garlic
1 tsp. basil
1 pkg. peppered ham, chopped, or 2 cups fresh boiled
    and peeled shrimp

Bring chicken broth and water to a boil, and add salt and grits, stirring slowly to prevent lumps. Reduce to low heat and simmer for five minutes, stirring occasionally. Remove from heat, add cheese, and stir until cheese is completely melted. Season with dash or two of Tabasco. Add butter, eggs, and milk one at a time, stirring to make sure that each is thoroughly blended. Fold in onions, garlic, basil, and ham or shrimp, and refrigerate overnight in plastic bowl. Next morning, preheat oven to 350 degrees, place grits mixture in individual ramekins, and bake for about 45 minutes or until set. Serves four to six.

Banana Bread Deluxe

$1/2$ **cup Crisco cooking oil**
$1^1/_2$ **cups sugar**
3 eggs, well beaten
$1/_4$ **tsp. salt**
$1^1/_2$ **cups flour, sifted**
1 tsp. baking soda
$1/_3$ **cup buttermilk**
4 large, ripe bananas, mashed
1 cup pecans, chopped

Cream oil and sugar, and add eggs and salt. Mix well. Add flour/soda and buttermilk alternately and stir in bananas. Fold in nuts and pour into loaf pan. Bake in preheated oven 45 minutes at 350 degrees.

The Oliver-Britt House
512 Van Buren Avenue
Oxford, MS 38655
662-234-8043
Fax: 662-281-8065

Five rooms with private baths in circa-1905 two-story red brick Greek Revival structure. Some antique furnishings. Cable TV in rooms, phone in upstairs hall. Full Southern breakfast. Children welcome, no smoking, no pets. Reservation deposit required. Innkeepers Glynn Oliver and Mary Ann Britt. Rates $45-$65, extra person $10. AX, DS, MC, V. Pays commission to travel agents.

The Oliver-Britt House was built in 1905, and a Doctor Guyton had an eye clinic here in the 1920s. It remained an eye clinic until 1982, when the present owners bought it for their bed and breakfast inn. Our upstairs room was small but comfortably furnished with a queen-size bed. We were reminded of a hotel room we once had in Scotland, or maybe some of the accommodations at College Hall at the University of London.

When we arrived, a large yellow cat was asleep in one of the comfortable lobby chairs. He did not speak, but we assumed that he had handled our reservations, since we saw no one else. Our room key and instructions were on the large center table, and our room was ready.

We learned better the next morning. Breakfast is ordinarily served at 8:30 on Sunday, but we were trying to get off early, so Ilean, the cook and manager, brought us cereal, toast, tea, and juice. She told us if we had time to wait she would soon have a full breakfast of cheese grits, bacon, and eggs prepared. We thanked her, but settled for the raisin bran.

Puddin Place
1008 University Avenue
Oxford, MS 38655
662-234-1250

Two suites with private baths in restored circa-1892 Victorian home. Antique furnishings. TV, phone in hall, fireplaces. Full breakfast. Children welcome, no smoking, no pets. Innkeeper Ann Turnbow. Rates $95. No credit cards. Pays commission to travel agents.

A working fireplace in every room, including even a bathroom, makes Puddin Place unique in our experience. Ann Turnbow also provides wood and starter material. Her two suite accommodations are large enough that no one gets claustrophobia here.

The Victorian-style home is loaded with antiques, and the decor includes handmade quilts. An inviting back porch with swing, rockers, and chairs provides a perfect spot for guests to gather in the mornings or afternoons. Puddin Place's location on University Avenue is ideal for those attending football games and other functions at Ole Miss. One just drives straight down the street to the university.

Ann does a lot of different things for breakfast, such as Baked French Toast, Pineapple Muffins, and Breakfast Parfaits, and she has provided some recipes.

Apple French Toast

1 cup brown sugar
⅓ cup margarine
2 tbsp. white corn syrup
1 apple
4 slices (¾" thick) French bread
5 eggs
1½ cups milk
1 tsp. vanilla

Put brown sugar, margarine and corn syrup in an 8"x 8" Pyrex container. Microwave until margarine melts and mix to form paste in bottom of Pyrex. Place 3 or 4 slices of cored apple rings on top of paste. Loosely place French bread on top of this in a single layer. Cut bread to fit. Do not pack tightly.

In a mixing bowl, whisk eggs, milk, and vanilla, and pour over French bread. Cover and refrigerate overnight. Uncover and bake 40 minutes at 350 degrees. Allow to cool a few minutes and carefully invert onto a platter. Surround with bacon and/or sausage. Top with additional apple rings if desired. Makes four generous servings.

Individual Ham Sandwich Casserole

Cooking spray
2 slices bread with crusts removed
Hot-pepper jack cheese
Swiss cheese
Shaved ham
1 egg
¼ cup half-and-half
Salt, pepper, and paprika to taste
Parsley

Spray individual baking ramekin with cooking spray. Put slice of bread in bottom and layer with cheeses and ham. Top with remaining slice of bread. Whisk together egg, half-and-half, and seasonings. Pour over bread, being sure to saturate the top slice. Bake at 350 degrees until lightly brown, about 30 minutes. Sprinkle with parsley and serve.

PASS CHRISTIAN

During the Civil War, there was a skirmish at Pass Christian on April 4, 1862, the day after one in Biloxi, and then on June 22, the same year, a Union raid took place here.

Today, Pass Christian is a town of stately mansions overlooking sand beaches along the gulf shore. Many of these large houses were built as summer homes by wealthy New Orleans people who fled to the coast to escape summer heat and

humidity, yellow fever, and malaria. Ancient live oaks and magnolias are interspersed with camellias and azaleas that are old
in their own right.

Pass Christian's yacht harbor is one of the most picturesque
along the coast, with scores of motor- and sailboats tied up at
the docks or moving in and out. It is a great place to watch the
boat traffic. In May the Blessing of the Fleet is held here, and in
December they celebrate with Christmas in the Pass. There are
several restaurants, including Annie's, specializing in steak and
seafood and Café de Soleil, a coffeehouse that also serves sandwiches, soups, and croissants. The regulars here like the curry
tuna salad.

Hillyer House is probably the most popular shopping place
in town since it features the works of more than 175 artists,
potters, and jewelers from all over the United States. Lonesome
Duck Stables, a private recreational area, is also located in Pass
Christian and has a nature trail, picnic areas, and horse rentals.
For golfers there is semiprivate,18-hole Pass Christian Isles Golf
Club.

Harbour Oaks Inn
126 West Scenic Drive
Pass Christian, MS 39571
1-800-452-9399 or 228-452-9399
Fax: 228-452-9200

*Five rooms with private baths in 1860 three-story National Register
property. Antique furnishings. TV, phone, kitchen access (microwave
and refrigerator—no cooking), billiard room. Full Southern breakfast.
Complimentary wine, soft drinks, and snacks. Children over 12 only,
no smoking in rooms, call about pets. Reservation deposit required.
Seven-day cancellation policy for weekends, 24-hour for weekdays, $15
cancellation fee charged. Innkeepers Tony and Diane Brugger. Rates
$83-$118. Senior discount. MC, V. Pays commission to travel agents.*

Directly across from the Pass Christian Yacht Harbor, this inn
is aptly named. Harbour Oaks Inn is the only 19th-century
hotel remaining from an era when the Mississippi coast was
known as the American Riviera. Its National Register plaque
identifies it as the Crescent Hotel.

In its earliest days, however, the property was called Live Oak House. There is a story that the 1860 building was used as a Confederate hospital during Union bombardment of the harbor. It received the Crescent Hotel name sometime after the Civil War, when it was purchased by a man from New Orleans. During most of the 20th century Harbour Oaks was a private residence but with parts of it often rented out as apartments. Twice the Pass Christian Yacht Club used it as a temporary clubhouse, the last time being when theirs was destroyed by Hurricane Camille in the 1960s.

The antebellum structure became Harbour Oaks Inn in 1921 when renovation began, a project that is ongoing, according to innkeeper Tony Brugger. In the 1930s when the Dodge family owned the place (the automobile Dodge family), Katharine Hepburn and John Ford were guests. Tony says he is a Southerner—southern Wisconsin—and he prepares breakfast once a week, with banana fritters being one of his specialties. The rest of the time, guests get a coupon good at a nearby restaurant, and the offerings are still Southern.

Inn at the Pass
125 East Scenic Drive
Pass Christian, MS 39571
1-800-217-2588 or 228-452-0333
E-mail: InnatPas@aol.com
Web site: www.Innatpass.com

Inn at the Pass

*One cottage behind, and five rooms with private baths in circa-1885
National Register home facing the Gulf of Mexico. Antique furnishings.
Cable TV, phone available, microwave, refrigerator, coffeemaker,
washer/dryer. Full breakfast. Call about children, smoking on porch, no
pets. Walk-ins accepted, but reservation recommended with 10-day cancellation policy and cancellation fee charged. Innkeepers Phyllis Hines
and Mimi Smith. Rates $85-$115, extra person $10. All major credit
cards. Pays commission to travel agents.*

The present Inn at the Pass is the second house to occupy
this site. An antebellum home was destroyed by fire in 1877.
The house that stands here now was built by the Butcher family,
merchants who came to Pass Christian from Alsace-Lorraine in
France about 1860. When the Butchers suffered financial
reversals in 1904, Emile J. Adam and his wife, Mattie, bought
the home.

Adam was editor of the local newspaper, and in the 39 years
that he stayed here he was a lawyer, federal marshal, mayor of
Pass Christian, and president of the board of supervisors of
Harrison County. In all, four generations of the Adam family
lived here for more than 76 years. It became a bed and breakfast in 1994, and the current proprietors, sisters Mimi Smith
and Phyllis Hines, are Mississippi Gulf Coast natives.

The owners are in the process of redecorating the rooms,
and even though they all have private baths, two are not *en suite*.
The Hunt Room has a half-bath in the room and a shower
nearby, and the Magnolia Room has an adjoining private bath.
The cottage, located at the back of the garden, has one bedroom and a bath and is furnished with two queen-size beds plus
sofa, refrigerator, toaster, and coffeemaker.

PORT GIBSON

When he occupied Port Gibson during the Civil War, Gen. U.
S. Grant thought it "too beautiful to burn" and spared it from
the Union torch. The small Mississippi town, situated on Bayou
Pierre between Vicksburg and Natchez, was first chartered in
1803 as Gibson's Landing, the seat of Claiborne County. The
stately old homes that line its streets continue to reflect the

charm that Grant saw and felt. Among the many historic build-ings is the First Presbyterian Church, famous for its spire topped with a gilded hand, forefinger pointing heavenward. The oldest Jewish synagogue in Mississippi is being restored here, and plans call for it to become a museum.

Several miles northwest and very near the Mississippi River, Grand Gulf Military Park is where Confederate troops tem-porarily held off a Union army and navy bent on subduing Vicksburg and gaining control of the Mississippi. The park has the remains of old rifle pits and gun emplacements, and a small museum on the grounds is filled with memorabilia of the Civil War here. Other sights of interest in the area include the Shaifer House, scene of one of the battles, and the stark ruins of Windsor, a once-proud mansion that burned in 1890, leaving only its columns standing as a reminder of its past.

For more information, contact the Port Gibson Chamber of Commerce, Highway 61 South, P.O. Box 491, Port Gibson, MS 39150, 601-437-4351. They are open Monday-Friday from 8 to 4, Saturday from 9 to 4, Sunday from noon to 4, but closed week-ends during December and January.

Oak Square Country Inn
1207 Church Street
Port Gibson, MS 39150
1-800-729-0240 or 601-437-4350

Twelve rooms with private baths in 1850 National Register Greek Revival mansion and adjacent guesthouses. Antique furnishings, fam-ily pieces. TV, phone, canopied beds. Tour included. Full Southern

Oak Square Country Inn
Illustration by Rubia Sherry

breakfast. Call about children, smoking restricted, no pets. Innkeeper
Martha B. Lum. Rates $85-$105, extra person $20. AX, DS, MC, V.
Pays commission to travel agents.

Once the home of a cotton planter, Oak Square is the most
palatial mansion in Port Gibson. The grounds feature a courtyard, fountain, and gazebo, as well as the massive oaks from
which the house takes its name. Six fluted Corinthian columns
accent the front gallery, which leads into an entrance hall with
a magnificent stairway.

Five of the units are located in a two-story white brick townhouse, complete with decorative iron columns, facing the street
directly behind the main house. Mrs. Lum said that it is an
exact replica of one in the New Orleans French Quarter.

Furnishings include a secretary attributed to famous New
Orleans craftsman Prudent Mallard, a rare Chickering piano,
and a beautiful array of silver, china, and crystal. You might
even get to sleep in the bed that belonged to Mrs. Lum's great-
grandparents. In fact, any bed you sleep in will likely be an
antique family piece from either her side of the family or that of
her late husband, Bill.

This was one of the first American bed and breakfast inns
we ever spent the night in, and it remains a favorite of ours.
We did sleep in the bed of Martha's great-grandparents, and we
treasure the experience. This gracious innkeeper seems to do
everything right.

After a full country breakfast of eggs, grits, sausage, bacon,
biscuits, jelly or preserves, juice, and coffee—and with some
instructions from the owner—you are well fortified for a tour of
Port Gibson and its surroundings.

SENATOBIA

Founded in 1860, Senatobia boomed in the 1870s with the
coming of the railroad. The town contains several unique shops
that draw visitors from all over the United States. The Loft is a
high-end purveyor of Western furnishings, and Petite Shop
attracts a dainty female clientele. The Tate County Courthouse,
circa 1875, is designated a Mississippi Landmark and is one of
the 10 most historic courthouses in the state.

For additional information, contact the Tate County Economic Development Foundation/Tourism, 662-562-8715, fax: 662-562-5786.

Spahn House
401 College Street
Senatobia, MS 38668
1-800-400-9853 or 662-562-9853
Fax: 662-562-8160
Web site: www.spahnhouse.com

Four rooms, two with whirlpool baths, in circa-1904 two-story Greek Revival mansion. Antique furnishings. TV, phone available. Honeymoon package. Full Southern breakfast. Lunch or dinner available. No children, smoking restricted, no pets. Reservation deposit required. Innkeeper Daughn Spahn. Rates $75-$110. Corporate discount. AX, MC, V. Pays commission to travel agents.

Spahn House, located in the National Register Historic District of Senatobia, was originally Victorian, but a later owner decided to give it a Greek Revival look and did so by changing the facade, adding four two-story columns across the front. The 5,000-square-foot home has 15 rooms, including six bedrooms and six and a half baths. Ceilings downstairs are 12 feet and those upstairs 11 feet. Innkeeper Daughn Spahn and husband Joe, who is a building contractor, took over the house in 1994

Spahn House

after it had been vacant for 22 years. During this time the owners had attempted to maintain it, but the Spahns found a total restoration necessary.

Daughn, who is vice-president of the Mississippi Bed and Breakfast Association, caters all sorts of functions, including showers, luncheons, weddings, anniversaries, and candlelight dinners for two. The latter are quite popular, she says, and she adds that she will serve whatever the client desires, from lobster to chili.

The rooms are all furnished with antiques, and the innkeeper notes that she and Joe have slept in every guestroom to test comfort and convenience. A suit of armor draped with lights stands on the stair landing. Daughn says that he had occupied various spots in the house before she gave Sir Henry—his name—the job of lighting the staircase. He is also known as the "Knight Light."

One of the bathrooms contains an old penny scale. The hostess notes that it stood downstairs for several years because it was so heavy. She finally got three workmen to move it to its present spot, which she says is permanent.

Guests, many of whom are businesspeople, have the full use of two common areas. Of the six and a half baths, the Spahns added three. Joe says that the one that gave him the most trouble was in the bedroom directly above the parlor. Known as the Red Room, this unit proved troublesome because he did not want to damage or change the parlor ceiling. Persistence paid off, however, and he managed to get a nice facility into a small space. He did settle for a shower, instead of tub and shower, however.

SHELBY

Incorporated in 1903, Shelby was named for a doctor and had previously been known as Belle View. It has always been a farming town, and today, with a population of about 3,800, it remains a center of cotton and rice farming. Shelby Homecoming is its only major event and is held in May every year near Memorial Day.

Bailwood Bed & Breakfast
Illustration by Lyle
Dilworth

Bailwood Bed & Breakfast
705 Highway 61 North
Shelby, MS 38774
662-398-5758

Three rooms with shared bath in 1891 two-story Greek Revival home. Antique furnishings. TV, phone available. Full breakfast. In-house tea-room provides lunch at extra charge. Children welcome, no smoking, no alcohol, no pets except in outside dog yard. Innkeepers Mr. and Mrs. Wallace Bailey. Rates $59.50. Extended-stay discount. No credit cards.

Mrs. Bailey was cooking lunch when we arrived, and since it was Friday, her menu was beef stew or chicken tenders, ranch potatoes, squash dressing, baked tomatoes, and cornbread. For dessert there was a choice of coconut or chocolate pudding cake. Mrs. Bailey rotates her weekday menus with other entrees including chicken and dumplings, meatloaf, hamburger steak, and chicken spaghetti Rotel. She also serves a variety of sandwiches, salads, and soups. Even though she was busy, she found time to show us through the old Greek Revival home.

Bailwood has had only three owners. The founder of the town, a Mr. Connell, built it; Mable Sherbaum was the second owner in 1946; and the Baileys have been here since 1992, with five years spent restoring the place. Wallace is vice-president of the physical plant at Delta State University in Cleveland, and she is retired from Dr. Hollingsworth's clinic.

STARKVILLE

Starkville is the home of Mississippi State University, largest in the state and noted for its agricultural research. The A. B. McKay Laboratory offers wine-tasting tours by appointment, and the dairy plant makes and sells red-wax-wrapped Mississippi Edam cheese. It was known as Boardtown when it was founded in 1831 but was later renamed for Gen. John Stark, a Revolutionary War hero. The town is the seat of Oktibbeha County, which was originally Choctaw land and means "icy water."

The first whites to settle here were Presbyterian missionaries led by Cyrus Kingbury. In 1820 this group developed Mayhew Mission in the northeast corner of the county, where they built a school, gristmill, blacksmith shop, and several other structures. Soon after, Calvin Cushman established another mission at Hebron, about three miles northwest of present-day Starkville. Converting the Indian trails into wagon roads, the missionaries made the area more accessible to traffic, and the first public road in the county was Robinson Road, constructed with federal and state funds in the early 1820s.

With the Treaty of Dancing Rabbit Creek, the Choctaws gave up their land here in 1830 in exchange for land in Oklahoma. White settlers poured in to fill the vacuum left by the Indians' departure, many of them attracted to this area by two large springs.

The first courthouse was a one-room log building, and the jail had no doors or windows. Prisoners were let down into it by rope. Following the Presbyterians came the Methodists and the Baptists, and a local lawyer named David Ames started a school in the log courthouse. The area developed into small farms, with a few large plantations.

The Civil War and Reconstruction were painful for Starkville, but in the 1870s the first railroad came in. Fire destroyed the town in 1875, but they rebuilt. Today Starkville is rapidly growing in agriculture and industry and expanding the university. Special events include an International Fiesta and an Arts Festival, both in April.

For more information, contact the Starkville Visitors and Convention Council, 322 University Drive, Starkville, MS 39759, 1-800-649-8687.

Carpenter Place

Carpenter Place
1280 Highway 25 South
Starkville, MS 39759
662-323-4669

Two rooms upstairs in main house with private baths, plus a suite in the Carriage House with two rooms and a bath in circa-1835 National Register property. Antique furnishings. TV, phone available. Tours $5 per person. Full Southern breakfast. No children, no smoking, no pets. Reservation deposit required. Innkeepers Dr. Roy E. and Lucy Carpenter. Rates $75-$150. MC, V.

We called innkeeper Lucy Carpenter on our cell phone to get directions. As this led us into a handsome subdivision of contemporary homes, we began to wonder, but the grouped houses and paved streets gave way to a dirt track leading uphill to the beautiful grandeur of 1835 Carpenter Place. Lucy gave us a tour, pointing out that husband Roy is a descendant of the original owners and was in fact reared in the house. All of the antique furnishings are family pieces from either his or her side.

The house dominates its surrounding 140 acres, where guests may wander to their hearts' content and maybe see an occasional deer or other wildlife. Carpenter Place once made its livelihood from dairying, and Lucy told us that some of the first Jersey cattle brought to Mississippi were brought here.

A recent ice storm had given the couple some heartbreaking problems, including the loss of a magnificent old oak. But the cleanup was under way, and the grounds were in much better condition than one would expect on a gray February day.

Two bedrooms in the main house are elegantly comfortable, as is the two-bedroom suite in the Carriage House. Lucy's breakfast may be anything from sausage casserole to Dutch babies to traditional Southern, and she has shared some recipes.

Dutch Babies

PANCAKE
⅓ cup butter
4 eggs, slightly beaten
1 cup milk
1 tsp. vanilla
1 cup flour
1 tsp. sugar
⅛ tsp. nutmeg

TOPPING
2 tbsp. powdered sugar
2 cups sliced fruit
½ cup whipped cream

Preheat oven to 425 degrees. Melt butter in large black skillet or four small skillets. Combine eggs, milk, vanilla, flour, sugar, and nutmeg, and pour into prepared pan(s). Bake for 20 minutes or until puffy. The pancake will rise, and when you remove it from the oven, the center will fall. Sprinkle with powdered sugar and add fruit and dollops of whipped cream. Serve immediately. Makes six to eight servings from large skillet or four from small ones.

Mama Lipsey's Biscuits

2 cups self-rising flour
¼ cup shortening
⅔-¾ cup buttermilk

Preheat oven to 500 degrees. Measure flour into bowl and make a hole in the center. Place shortening in hole. Mix with hand as you add buttermilk a little at a time. When thoroughly moist, place on floured board or waxed paper and knead only twice. Roll to ½" thickness. Using a floured biscuit cutter, cut biscuits without twisting. Place on greased baking sheet and bake 8 to 10 minutes. Butter as soon as you remove from oven. Makes a dozen 2" biscuits.

TUPELO

Most famous for being the birthplace of Elvis Presley, the rock and roll legend, Tupelo is also the site of the Civil War Battle of Tupelo. Presley was born in a two-room shotgun house but did not get to stay here long. After two years, his family was evicted because they could not pay the $180 they had borrowed to build the house. It is now part of the 15-acre park for disadvantaged children that was built with funds raised by Presley at a concert in Tupelo. A museum behind the house contains a variety of Elvis memorabilia including clothes and records.

The Tupelo National Battlefield covers the site of the fight between Union general A. J. Smith and Confederate general Nathan Bedford Forrest. The result was more of a standoff, with the Union troops retreating for lack of supplies and Forrest's men floundering because of a misunderstood direction.

Other sites include the Tupelo City Museum, which houses Indian artifacts and a Visitor Center on the Natchez Trace Parkway just north of town. The Lyric Theater on North Broadway has been restored and remodeled to present live productions four times a year plus a Christmas Show, Winter Dinner Theater, and Summer Youth Program.

For additional information, contact Tupelo Convention and Visitors Bureau, 399 East Main Street, P.O. Drawer 47, Tupelo, MS 38802, 1-800-533-0611 or 662-841-6521, Web site: www.tupelo.net.

The Mockingbird Inn Bed & Breakfast
305 North Gloster
Tupelo, MS 38676
662-841-0286
Fax: 662-840-4158
E-mail: sandbird@netdoor.com
Web site: www.bbonline.com/ms/mockingbird/

Seven rooms in two-story 1925 bungalow. Antique and contemporary furnishings. TV, VCR with free movies, phone. Whirlpool in Athens Room. Full breakfast. Restaurants nearby. Call about children, no smoking, pets $5. Reservation deposit required. Three-day cancellation policy

and cancellation fee charged. Innkeeper Jim Gilmer. Rates $65-$95,
Friday and Saturday $71-$125, extra person $10. Senior discount. AX,
DS, MC, V. Pays commission to travel agents.

Bungalow-style Mockingbird Inn was built in 1925 by depot
agent Douglas Potter and his wife, Mary Jane. Potter died of
pneumonia contracted when he saved a hobo from certain
death by pulling him off the tracks before an oncoming train.
Despite this unfortunate occurrence, the house remained in
the family for three generations.

The inn seems to have led a charmed life. It was one of very
few buildings to survive a devastating tornado that struck
Tupelo in 1936, and a severe ice storm in 1994 left most of the
town without electricity for days—but not Mockingbird Inn. In
other incarnations, the bungalow has been cut into apartments,
served as a pool and patio store, and operated as a clothing
boutique. The house even has an Elvis connection of sorts. The
celebrated rock and roll star once attended the Milam School
across the street.

We were given the tour by amiable Jonathan Sloan, and the
themed accommodations are unique in our experience. The
innkeepers have adopted favorite travel spots as their decor.
The Venice Room features an 1800s tapestry of gondolas on the
Grand Canal being poled past the Doge's Palace. The Athens
Room has an ell-shaped whirlpool for two reminiscent of the
Greek baths; a porch swing denotes the Mackinac Island Room;
Victorian-style wicker furniture sets the scene for the Paris
Room; light and airy is the only way to describe the Sanibel
Island Room; the Bavaria Room recalls winter sports with
antique skis and skates; and finally, there is the Africa Room
decorated with faux zebra and leopard skins.

Romance packages with long-stemmed roses and carriage
rides are available as is in-room massage therapy. Full breakfast
is served, but a lighter continental is served, too. A light
evening snack is also available, and several restaurants are
within walking distance.

VICKSBURG

First settled by the Spanish in 1790, Vicksburg was incorporated as such in 1825. Its major claim to fame was as the east-west linchpin of the Confederacy that withstood a 47-day siege by Union forces, finally surrendering to Gen. Ulysses S. Grant on July 4, 1863. Today, even though the town remains an important river port, handling over three million tons of cargo annually, its major industry is tourism. The Vicksburg National Military Park and the many restored antebellum and Victorian homes draw more than a million visitors a year, and gaming boats more than double this figure.

Two events left their marks on Vicksburg. In addition to the historic Civil War battle, the Mississippi changed its course and left the town high and dry in the later 1800s. This had serious consequences for the economy, since the town was a major river port. The problem was finally solved by diverting the Yazoo River through a series of lakes into the old Mississippi bed. With water at its feet once more, the Port of Vicksburg again became viable.

The earlier event draws tourists to the Vicksburg National Military Park, located in the northeast portion of the city. Including a visitor center with an interpretive film about the siege, and much of the old battleground, the park is laid out so you can take a 16-mile driving tour of the lines. Along the battlefield route, you will see strategic strongpoints of the Blue and the Gray, as well as state memorials, statues, and markers.

Many of the antebellum homes retain battle scars, with cannonballs embedded in their walls and floors. Some offer bed and breakfast, and the Spring Pilgrimage allows visitors to tour more of these historic structures, including the Martha Vick House, home of the daughter of the Methodist minister for whom the town is named.

Confederate soldiers once camped on the three-acre grounds of McRaven. Located at 1445 Harrison Street, the home, which was built in three stages and styles, is said to be the site of some of the heaviest fighting of the siege, and it has the battle scars to prove it. The periods and styles include the original 1797 brick, 1836 Empire, and 1849 Greek Revival. Today the grounds are used for battle reenactments. McRaven is open Monday-Saturday from 9 to 5 and Sunday from 10 to 5, but it is closed December through February. Admission is $5 for adults, $4 for groups of 10 or more, and free for under 12.

On the highest point in Vicksburg, the Old Court House now stands as a museum. It was here that Jefferson Davis began his political career, and it was also here that Grant reviewed his victorious troops. Today, its nine rooms and two hallways contain artifacts and memorabilia of its Southern heritage. On Washington Street, the Biedenharn Candy Company Museum marks the spot where Coca-Cola was first bottled, in 1894.

There are a number of good restaurants, including Walnut Hills, where weekdays at lunch you can sit with other diners at a large round table with a lazy Susan and help yourself to fried chicken, rice and gravy, turnip greens, cabbage, butter beans, black-eyed peas, squash, sweet potatoes, macaroni and cheese, coleslaw, potato salad, cornbread, biscuits, iced tea, and dessert.

Andre's at Cedar Grove is another good spot. On one trip here, we had an excellent dark-roux gumbo, a salad of crisp romaine, cucumbers, tomatoes, and croutons topped with the slightly sweet house dressing, and entrees of orange roughy and salmon. The roughy was topped with a shrimp sauce and the salmon with a caper one. The accompanying vegetable melange included a whole glazed carrot, small, whole crook-neck squash, zucchini sliced lengthwise, and fresh asparagus.

A loaf of warm bread spotted throughout with bits of sun-dried tomato was served with a plate of olive oil, sprinkled at the table with freshly ground black pepper and Parmesan cheese. Service was excellent; it may have been that it was a slow night, but the server, her assistant, the maitre d', and maybe even the dishwasher were constantly attending to our needs— all addressing us by name, i.e., Mr. and Mrs. Baldwin.

The riverboats with their wide-open gambling have added another facet to Vicksburg. They provide round-the-clock entertainment with their casinos and with various celebrity appearances that the boats sponsor.

For more information, contact the Vicksburg Convention and Visitors Bureau, corner of Clay and Old Highway 27, P.O.

Box 110, Vicksburg, MS 39181, 1-800-221-3536 or 601-636-9421,
Web site: www.vicksburg.org/cvb.

Anchuca
1010 First East Street
Vicksburg, MS 39180
1-800-262-4822 or 601-636-4931

Five rooms and two corporate apartments, all with private baths, in
1830 National Register Greek Revival mansion and dependencies.
Period furnishings. TV, phone available, swimming pool, whirlpool, dec-
orative fireplaces. Full Southern breakfast. Tours, afternoon tea, and
honor bar. Caters luncheons, dinners, and parties. Call about children,
some nonsmoking rooms, no pets. Reservation deposit required. 72-hour
cancellation policy. Innkeeper Loveta Byrne. Rates $85-$190, extra
person $20. All major credit cards. Pays commission to travel agents.

There have been some changes at Anchuca, primarily a
change of ownership. Loveta Byrne, previously of the Burn in
Natchez, has replaced May C. Burns as proprietor and
innkeeper. Located in the heart of the Vicksburg Historic
District, Anchuca takes its name from an Indian word that
means "happy home," and the 1830 Greek Revival structure was
once the residence of Jefferson Davis's brother. On one occasion, the Confederate president addressed Vicksburg citizens
from the second-floor balcony that projects above the double
entrance doors of the colonnaded front. Landscaped gardens
and brick courtyards complement the two-story antebellum
home.

Inside, elaborate chandeliers still hang from the ceilings, and
period furnishings decorate the rooms. Of the units available to
guests, two are in the main house, two corporate apartments
are in the restored slave quarters, and three accommodations
are in the 1900 guesthouse. A hot tub in an indoor-outdoor
cabana is adjacent to the swimming pool.

After early-morning coffee in a brick courtyard, visitors are
served breakfast in the formal dining room of the mansion.
The full Southern meal may include hot homemade bread, cof-
feecake, pancakes, cheese grits, fruit, juice, and coffee.

One thing that has not changed is Julia Dunbar. The housekeeper has been at Anchuca since 1972, and she provided the following recipes.

Overnight Coffeecake

¾ cup softened margarine
1 cup sugar
2 eggs
8 oz. sour cream
2 cups plain flour
1 tsp. baking powder
1 tsp. baking soda
½ tsp. salt
1 tsp. ground nutmeg
¾ cup firmly packed brown sugar
½ cup chopped pecans
1 tsp. ground cinnamon

Combine margarine and sugar. Cream until light and fluffy. Add eggs and sour cream, mixing well. Combine next 5 ingredients; add to batter and mix well. Pour into a greased and floured 13" x 9" x 2" baking pan.

Combine brown sugar, pecans, and cinnamon. Mix well. Sprinkle evenly over batter. Cover and chill in refrigerator overnight. Uncover and bake at 350 degrees for 35-40 minutes.

Bourbon Pie

½ pkg. Famous chocolate wafers
3 tbsp. butter, melted
1 small can evaporated milk
21 large marshmallows
½ pt. whipping cream
3 tbsp. bourbon

Roll wafers into crumbs and mix with melted butter. Save ½ cup of crumbs for topping. Spread balance of crumbs evenly in pie pan and bake for 5 minutes in 350-degree oven. Cool. Mix eaporated milk with marshmallows in double boiler and heat over hot, not boiling, water until smooth, stirring until well mixed. Cool over a bowl of ice. Whip cream and add bourbon. Fold into cooled marshmallow mixture and pour into pie shell. Sprinkle reserved crumbs on top. Chill thoroughly.

Annabelle Bed & Breakfast
501 Speed Street
Vicksburg, MS 39180
1-800-791-2000 or 601-638-2000
Fax: 601-636-5054

Five rooms with private baths and one two-room suite with bath in circa-1868 two-story Victorian-Italianate home and guesthouse in historic Garden District. Period family furnishings. Cable TV, phone, swimming pool. Full Southern breakfast. Children over six or infants in arms only, no smoking, no pets. Reservation deposit required. Innkeeper Carolyn C. Mayer. Rates $85-$125. AX, DS, MC, V. Pays commission to travel agents.

John Klein was married to a cousin of Union general William Tecumseh Sherman, and the couple had 10 children, six of whom lived to adulthood. In 1868 he built this brick Victorian-Italianate mansion on the grounds of his Cedar Grove estate for his son Madison Conrad Klein. Carolyn and George Mayer have been providing bed and breakfast in this historic Garden District property since 1992, and they named it for the Annabelles in three generations of her family.

Carolyn is from New Orleans, and George first saw light of day in Moravia in the Czech Republic. Incidentally, his great-great-grandfather was once mayor of Prague. When we arrived

Annabelle Bed & Breakfast

at about 3, Carolyn was outside watering her flowers, but she immediately came inside and served us tea and homemade cookies from a silver tray in her formal living room.

Many of the antiques that fill the home are family pieces. Included among these was a cockfight chair—something we had never seen before. It is made to be straddled backward and has a padded rest across the top of the back, which opens to provide a compartment for keeping money while betting on the birds.

We stayed in the Rose room, the others in the main house being the Peach and the Magnolia, where guests can view blooming magnolia trees. The Gardenia, the Camellia, and the Natchez Suite are located in the guesthouse on the grounds. This Queen Anne-style guesthouse was moved from Pearl Street in 1881 on a mule-drawn wagon, according to Carolyn. The Mayers added porches and columns.

A typical breakfast here can include eggs Benedict, omelet, French toast, homemade banana bread, fresh fruit, juice, and coffee or tea. Carolyn furnished us a nonbreakfast recipe, which follows.

Crab and Artichoke Annabelle

½ cup chopped green onion
3 tbsp. chopped parsley
1 clove garlic, minced
¼ cup extravirgin olive oil
1 tbsp. all purpose flour
¾ cup milk with Tabasco to taste
1 can large chopped artichoke hearts
1 lb. white lump crabmeat (fresh, if possible)
½ cup grated sharp cheddar cheese
½ cup grated Parmesan cheese

Sauté onions, parsley, and garlic in oil. Do not brown. Add flour and blend in. Stir in milk gradually. Gently fold in artichoke hearts. When blended, very gently fold in crabmeat. Place in a casserole and sprinkle on the cheeses. Bake 15 minutes at 325 degrees.

Balfour House

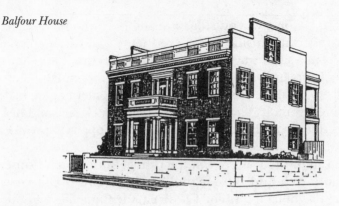

Balfour House
1002 Crawford Street
P.O. Box 1541
Vicksburg, MS 39181
1-800-294-7113 or 601-638-7113
Fax: 601-638-8484
Web site: www.balfourhouse.com

*Three rooms with private baths in 1835 Greek Revival National
Register home. Antique Empire furnishings. TV, phone. On-street parking. Tour included. Full breakfast. Caters wedding receptions and private parties. Children welcome, no smoking, pets welcome. Credit card
required for reservation. Innkeeper Sharon Humble. Rates $85-$150,
extra person $20. 10 percent senior discount. AX, MC, V. Pays com-
mission to travel agents.*

In 1862, a gala Christmas Eve ball at Balfour House was interrupted by news of the arrival of Federal gunboats above
Vicksburg. This was the beginning of the struggle that would
culminate in a 47-day siege of the city, ending July 4, 1863.
Emma Balfour kept a diary of events during the battle for the
river port, and toward the end, she noted, "All night they have
fired so that our poor soldiers have no rest and as we have few
reserves, it is very hard on them." Eventually, her home became
headquarters for Yankee occupation forces, and artifacts of that
fierce struggle are on display in the mansion today, including
an old cannonball found in the wall during restoration.

The red brick structure with its white, columned facade was

built by William Bobb in 1835 and sold to Dr. and Mrs. William Balfour in 1850. The three-story elliptical spiral staircase in the hall is said to be one of only three in the United States. The parlor features Empire furniture, and a bedroom on tour contains a massive seven-by-eight-foot canopied "family bed."

During the annual Spring Pilgrimage, on the second December Saturday, and at other times for special groups, a reenactment of the fateful 1862 ball at Balfour House takes place. Perhaps these festivities stir the ghosts of that long-ago party.

Belle of the Bends
508 Klein Street
Vicksburg, MS 39180
1 800-844-2308 or 601-634-0737
Web site: www.belleofthebends.com

Six rooms with private baths—three rooms have whirlpools, four have river view, two have kitchens—in 1876 three-story Victorian-Italianate home. Period furnishings. TV/VCR, tape library, phone. Full country breakfast. Fruit in room on request, afternoon tea. Children welcome, no smoking, no pets. Credit card required for reservation. Innkeepers Wally and Jo Pratt. Rates $95-$135, extra person $20. AX, DS, MC, V. Pays commission to travel agents.

Belle of the Bends
Illustration by Anne Dennis

On a bluff overlooking the Mississippi River, Belle of the Bends was built by state senator Murray F. Smith and his wife, Kate. Slender columns support the upper and lower verandas that wrap around three sides of the mansion and offer splendid river views to guests. Owner Jo Pratt relates that she named the house for a steamboat owned by her grandfather, Capt. Tom Morrissey. He ran the vessel as an excursion boat from New Orleans to Vicksburg, and on one occasion had Pres. Theodore Roosevelt as a passenger.

The home is filled with period furniture, Oriental rugs, and steamboat memorabilia. Breakfasts here are sumptuous and include omelets (made with egg substitutes if you so request upon arrival), eggs in ramekins, blueberry pancakes, and fresh apple muffins, for which Jo has shared the recipe.

Fresh Apple Muffins

1 cup sugar
2 tsp. cinnamon
2 tsp. baking soda
2 cups plain flour
$\frac{1}{2}$ tsp. salt
$\frac{1}{2}$ cup oil
2 tsp. vanilla
1 egg
4 cups diced apples
1 cup raisins
1 cup chopped nuts
Baking spray

Sift together dry ingredients. Add oil, vanilla, egg, and mix. Stir in apples, raisins, and nuts. Spoon into muffin tins coated with baking spray, and bake 20-25 minutes at 325 degrees. Makes 42 muffins.

Cedar Grove Mansion Inn
2200 Oak Street
Vicksburg, MS 39180
1- 800-862-1300 or 601-636-1000
Fax: 601-634-6126

Cedar Grove Mansion Inn
Illustration by Rubia Sherry

Thirty rooms with private baths in 1840 National Historic Landmark. Antique and period furnishings. TV, phone, swimming pool, whirlpool, bicycle, exercise room, tennis, croquet, gift shop. Full Southern breakfast. Complimentary tea. Dinner available. Mansion Bar, Andre's Restaurant. Call about children, no smoking, no pets. Credit card required for reservation. Innkeepers Ted and Estelle Mackey, general manager Rhonda Abraham. Rates $85-$165. Winter and senior discounts. AX, DS, MC, V. Pays commission to travel agents.

Built in 1840 by lumber and cotton baron John A. Klein as a wedding present for his bride, Cedar Grove became a Vicksburg showplace with elegant furniture and a ballroom fit for a president—Confederate, that is. Jefferson Davis once danced here. The mansion was damaged by fire from Union gunboats during the siege of the city, and a cannonball is still lodged in the parlor wall. Since the house later served the Federal troops as a hospital, perhaps the ghost of some Yankee soldier wanders about the grounds.

Many of the antique furnishings are original to the home, as are the gas chandeliers that hang in the rooms. Accommodations are in the main house, carriage house, poolside guesthouse, and Cottage Row across from the mansion. A rooftop observation deck with chairs and benches provides entrancing river views. The four acres of grounds include court-yards, fountains, gazebos, and a small family burial plot where the Kleins were first laid to rest. They were moved to the Vicksburg City Cemetery in 1960.

The full Southern breakfast—often scrambled eggs, golden grits, butter-soaked biscuits, sausage, orange juice, and coffee— is served in the garden room or outdoors, depending on the weather. Drinks are available at popular prices.

Cherry Street Cottage and Annex
2212 Cherry Street
Vicksburg, MS 39180
1-800-636-7086 or 601-636-7086
Fax: 601-629-9285

Four units with private baths in three cottages behind 1907 National Register home. Antique furnishings, collectibles, family pieces. TV, phone. Full Southern or heart-healthy breakfast. Call about children, no smoking, pets welcome. Innkeeper Betty Barnes Jackson. Rates $70-$100, extra person $20. All major credit cards.

The two-story brick house with a hipped red-tile roof, to which the Cherry Street Cottages are adjacent, was built in 1907 by wealthy wholesale grocer and cotton factor D. J. Schlenker in a combination prairie/bungalow style. Current owner Betty Jackson stresses, "We are turn-of-the-century and not antebellum," and adds that the guest quarters out back provide privacy in a relaxed atmosphere.

The one-bedroom Schlenker and Rose cottages have full kitchens with microwaves and, with a sofa bed, accommodate four people each. The two-unit Flora Cottage is in a turn-of-the-century duplex and also has a full kitchen (shared), two baths, and a washer/dryer. Furnishings include antiques, family pieces, and items that Betty has collected over the years.

The hostess likes to visit with her guests as they breakfast in the main house dining room. As she says, it can be "full cholesterol" or heart healthy; visitors decide. Many times the healthy variety features bran-banana muffins and the Southern-version Cheese Grits Soufflé, for which she has provided the recipe.

Cheese Grits Soufflé

1 cup grits
4 cups water
3 eggs, separated
2 tbsp. flour
1 tbsp. butter or margarine, melted
1½ cups milk
1 cup grated cheddar cheese
1 cup grated garlic cheese

Cook grits in boiling water and cool slightly. Beat egg yolks and gradually add some of grits to them. Add this mixture back to remaining grits. Blend flour into butter and stir in milk. Cook over low heat, stirring constantly, to make thin white sauce. Add cheeses to sauce, reserving a small amount of cheese for topping. Add sauce to grits. Beat egg whites stiffly and fold into mixture. Place in buttered 3-qt. dish and sprinkle with reserved cheese. Bake in 350-degree oven for 30 minutes or until puffy. Serves 12. May be prepared in individual ramekins. Can be frozen uncooked.

The Corners
601 Klein Street
Vicksburg, MS 39180
1-800-444-7421 or 601-636-7421

Fifteen units with private baths in 1872 National Register Louisiana raised cottage, servants' quarters, adjacent dependency, and two-story 1870s cottage across the street. Antique and period furnishings, handmade quilts. Cable TV, phone, fresh flowers, some whirlpools, some fireplaces. Tour included. Full Southern breakfast. Complimentary drinks. Children welcome, smoking on galleries, pets welcome. Reservation deposit required. Innkeeper Kilby Whitney. Rates $75-$150, $20 extra adult, $15 child 13-18, $10 under 13. All major credit cards. Pays commission to travel agents.

The Corners is a pleasing mix of Greek Revival and Italianate architecture with a floor plan that is a miniature replica of Cedar Grove. It was built as a wedding present for the daughter of Mr. and Mrs. John Klein when she married Isaac Bonham in 1873. The 68-foot gallery, with unusual pierced columns in club, diamond, heart, and spade designs, has high-back rockers and provides guests with a scenic view of the river and valley. The walkways of the parterre gardens are also available for relaxing strolls.

Seven rooms and a two-bedroom suite are in the main house, four bedrooms in the dependency, two in the servants' quarters, and there is a two-bedroom cottage across the street. Fresh flowers, sachets, and handmade quilts accent the antique furnishings that grace the accommodations. The dependency, which the Whitneys call the Galleries, is just north of the main house and is new since our last visit. The family is proud of the fact that they received an award from the Historical Society for the structure. Kilby says that it is a new building that from the outside looks like an old one.

Nine of the rooms have fireplaces, eight have whirlpools, and five have views of the river. At first glance, our upstairs room appeared to be windowless, but a closer look revealed a window that looked across a small hall to another window that gave us an outside view. The mattress on the massive four-poster bed was one of the most comfortable we have experienced, and there were nightstands with lamps on either side. We think that this is a major plus for any inn, because we often read and even write in bed.

The Corners serves a full plantation breakfast in the formal dining room on antique porcelain and silver, and guests have use of the library and double parlor. The Whitneys do not serve other meals, but there is an excellent restaurant just across the street at Cedar Grove.

Kilby has furnished two recipes from the Corners, which we are happy to share:

Virginia's Blueberry Banana Nut Muffins

2 eggs
1½ cups Canola oil
½ stick butter, melted
1½ cups sugar
1 banana, mashed

1 tbsp. vanilla
2½ cups self-rising flour
2½ cups oatmeal
1 cup buttermilk
2 cups blueberries
1½ cups chopped nuts

Mix eggs, oil, melted butter, and sugar. Add mashed banana and vanilla. Stir until firm. Add flour and oatmeal and moisten with all the buttermilk. Gently stir in blueberries and nuts. Spoon into three greased muffin tins. Bake at 350 degrees for 30 minutes or until slightly brown around the edges.

Overnight Caramel French Toast

1½ cups brown sugar
1½ sticks butter
1 tbsp. light corn syrup
8 slices French bread
8 eggs, beaten
2 cups milk
1½ tsp. vanilla
½ tsp. salt

Combine sugar, butter, and corn syrup in small saucepan. Cook over medium heat until thickened, stirring constantly. Pour syrup mixture into large rectangular Pyrex baking dish. Place bread on top of syrup mixture.

Combine eggs, milk, vanilla, and salt, stirring until blended. Pour egg mixture evenly over bread slices. Cover and chill 8 hours. Bake uncovered at 350 degrees for 45 minutes or until lightly browned. Remove from oven and turn upside down.

The Duff Green Mansion
1114 First East Street
Vicksburg, MS 39180
1-800-992-0037 or 601-636-6968
Fax: 601-661-0079

Seven units with private baths in three-story 1856 Palladian-style National Register mansion. Antique furnishings. TV, phone, swimming pool, working fireplaces, turndown service. Tour included. Full

Southern breakfast. Complimentary evening drinks. Ballroom available for parties and receptions. Children welcome, smoking outside, small pets welcome. Innkeeper Harry Sharp. Rates $85-$160, Jan.-Feb. $75-$140, extra adult $15. Senior discount. AX, MC, V. Pays commission to travel agents.

Located in the Vicksburg Historic District, the Duff Green Mansion is considered one of the best examples of Palladian architecture in Mississippi. The 12,000-square-foot home was built in 1856 by wealthy merchant Green for his bride, Mary Lake, on property given her as a wedding gift from her parents. Skilled slave labor was used to construct the three-story, double-galleried mansion adorned with lacy ironwork.

The home was shelled during the siege of Vicksburg, and, at one point when it was under attack, Mary gave birth to a son in a nearby cave shelter and called him Siege. Pressed into use as a hospital, the house provided medical care for both Confederate and Union soldiers until the end of the war.

The four units on the first floor are named Dixie, Camellia, Confederate, and Magnolia, and the three on the third floor are the Pemberton, Jeff Davis, and Duff Green suites. Of course, the Duff Green is the most elaborate, with a sitting area in the bedroom, queen sleeper sofa in the adjoining sitting room, and fireplaces in both. The dumbwaiter in the dining room is original to the house.

Today, guests enjoy the charm of an earlier time with modern conveniences. The B&B offers a swimming pool on the azalea-landscaped grounds, a complimentary evening drink, nightly turndown service, and a full Southern breakfast served in the dining room, gazebo, or guestrooms.

Floweree Cottage
2309 Pearl Street
Vicksburg, MS 39180
601-638-2704
Fax: 601-636-0052

Two units with private baths in guest cottage on grounds of 1870 National Register Italianate mansion. Period furnishings. TV, phone available, swimming pool. Full kitchen. Tour included. Full Southern

Floweree Cottage

breakfast. Complimentary beverages. Children over five only, smoking restricted, pets restricted. Credit card required for reservation. Innkeeper Gayle Tuminello. Rates $85-$110, extra person $20. Extended-stay discount. MC, V. Pays commission to travel agents.

Original owner Charles Floweree, for whom the main house was named, was the youngest colonel to serve in the Confederate army, according to Gayle Tuminello, current proprietor. By age 19, he had fought with Stonewall Jackson, helped lead Pickett's charge at Gettysburg, and been promoted to colonel at the Battle of the Pines. Toward the end of the war, the young colonel was captured and held prisoner until the latter part of July 1865.

Floweree came to Vicksburg in 1866, married, and went into the ice business with his father-in-law. Apparently he completed a home that had been begun during the war, and the result is the elaborate Italianate mansion the visitor sees today. Actually, the house, which is included in the Historic American Building Survey, was restored in 1961 by Gayle and architect husband Skip. Visitors will also enjoy the sculptured gardens and fountains.

Guest accommodations are in a cottage on the grounds of the main house, and the two two-bedroom units share a living room, dining room, and kitchen. Gayle likes to vary breakfast, ranging from traditional eggs, grits, and sausage to a Spanish omelet to an expanded continental, so that visitors do not have the same meal every morning.

The Stained Glass Manor—Oak Hall
2430 Drummond Street
Vicksburg, MS 39180
1-800-771-8893 or 601-638-8893
E-mail: vickbnb@magnolia.net
Web site: www.vickbnb.com

Five rooms with private baths in main house and one suite in carriage house of circa-1902-8 National Register home featuring 38 stained-glass windows. Eclectic furnishings. TV/VCR, phone jacks. Tours $5 adults, $3 children, $15 family maximum. Full New Orleans breakfast. Other meals by request. Children welcome, no smoking in rooms, call about pets. One-night reservation deposit required. $30 cancellation fee charged. Innkeepers Bill and Shirley Smollen. Rates $85-$185. Senior discount. AX, DS, MC, V. Pays commission to travel agents.

The home of Fannie Vick Willis Johnson was probably designed by George Washington Maher, known as the "father of indigenous American architecture." This is also known as the Prairie or Mission style, and in his early years, Frank Lloyd Wright was a student of Maher. The stained glass in the 38 windows is by Louis J. Millet, first dean of architecture at the University of Chicago and head of the Chicago Art Institute. After Fannie passed away in 1931, the house was used as a "widows" home by the Episcopal Diocese. The house was bought by Vicksburg mayor John Holland and his wife, Sarah, in 1966 and then passed through a series of hands. Bill and Shirley Smollen acquired the property in 1995 and renamed it the Stained Glass Manor—Oak Hall.

Bill was president of the Mississippi Bed and Breakfast Association when we visited and is quite an outgoing innkeeper. His rooms are named for presidents—Washington, Adams, Jefferson, Jackson, Polk, and, occasionally, Monroe, since this room is not always available. The carriage house has a large bedroom, sitting and dining areas, bath, and small kitchen.

The gourmet breakfast may include fresh baked bread, fresh, curried, or fermented fruit, juice, sausage, quiche Lorraine, or Chicken au Vin. The quiche recipe has been provided.

Quiche Lorraine
(Credited to late New Orleans restaurateur Al Masson)

5 lb. bacon
Butter
1 large or 2 medium onions, minced
1 pt. whipping cream
1 tbsp. ground nutmeg
1 tbsp. ground ginger
1 tbsp. dry mustard
5-6 drops Tabasco
6-10 eggs
1 block Swiss cheese, shredded
4-5 pie shells

Fry and drain bacon well on paper towels and crumble it. Sauté onions in butter until centers of pieces are clear and edges start to brown. Drain in strainer lined with paper towel. In large mixing bowl, whip cream, nutmeg, ginger, dry mustard, and Tabasco. Whip in the eggs, cheese, and cooled onion and bacon. Pour into pie shells and bake in a preheated oven at 375 degrees for 25-35 minutes. Place in gallon Ziploc freezer bags after cooling. Reheat at 375 degrees and serve with champagne, light Riesling, or orange juice. Serves 24 to 30.

WEST

The main street of this small Mississippi town of 184 people is Highway 51, and directly across from its two-block row of storefronts is the railroad, the reason for the town's existence in the first place. Many of the buildings are vacant, although one is modernized and occupied by a bank. Another is being restored by the West Historical and Preservation Society and will become a museum.

At its height, West was a thriving village of 500 or more people, but that was before the virgin timber was cut out, and when farming was still the primary livelihood of most Americans. Sadly, West fell to the economic realities that have been crippling if not fatal to much of small-town U.S.A. Yet the people here now like the pace of life and seem determined to keep it an attractive place to live.

The town has an extensive National Historic District with restored late-19th-century homes proudly bearing their names and dates. Only in 1998 did it see fit to hire a policeman, and that was to quell some vulgar language rather than deal with criminal activity. For those who are fascinated with small-town America, West is a place waiting to be discovered.

The Alexander House
210 Green Street
West, MS 39192
1-800-350-8034 or 662-967-2266

Five rooms and four baths in restored 1880 National Register property in National Historic District. Antique furnishings. TV in common room, phone available. Full Southern breakfast. Dinners and parties by reservation. Well-behaved children welcome, no smoking, call about pets. Innkeeper Ruth Ray Dinstell. Rates $65. AX, DS, MC, V. Pays commission to travel agents.

The Alexander House may have a ghost, or ghosts. Although innkeeper Ruth Ray Dinstell does not put much stock in the supernatural herself, she reports that guests and family members have detailed some strange happenings. Her rooms are named for the children of the Alexander family who occupied

The Alexander House

the house for many years even though they did not build it. Miss Annie was a maiden schoolteacher, and it has been in her room that most of the incidents have occurred.

On one occasion, one of Ruth Ray's daughters was helping her take down decorations in Miss Annie's room. The daughter was standing on the bed reaching up to remove a decoration from the wall when suddenly something or someone grabbed her hair in back and pulled. Ruth Ray's explanation was that the daughter must have caught her hair in her collar. The daughter pointed out that she was not wearing a collar, and she felt that for some reason Miss Annie did not approve of her activity.

Then, there is the case of the cat. Ruth Ray is a cat person, with five of her own (not at the B&B) and a cat motif throughout the Alexander House. Awhile back she bought a new wastebasket emblazoned with a wide-eyed cat, which she put in Miss Annie's room. Some guests from Georgia were there videotaping the entire house. When they pointed the camera at the trashcan, the cat blinked. Ruth Ray has the tape to prove it, but notes that it probably had something to do with the light.

Ruth Ray and her husband, Woody, have done an excellent job restoring and decorating the house in a style that could probably be called "Mississippi Country," although much of the furniture came from England, where they lived for five years. In addition to Miss Annie's room, there is Ulrich's and Dr. Joe's. Dr. Joe was educated as a dentist but never practiced because he decided he did not want to put his hands in other people's mouths. There is also a cottage behind the house that was once servant's quarters— a comfortable spot for two, but it will hold four.

Catering is a big part of the Alexander House amenities. Ruth Ray does steak dinners for a minimum of 10 at $25 a person. Her set menu is charcoal-grilled filet mignon, mushroom sauce with green pepper and onion, baked potato, green salad, fruit, garlic bread, Bananas Foster, tea, and coffee. A typical breakfast includes some sort of sweet pastry or homemade bread; bacon, ham, or sausage; eggs to order, French toast, or a casserole; fruit; biscuits; orange juice; and coffee or tea. She has furnished one of her recipes.

Raisin Bran Muffin Mix

1 15-oz. box raisin bran
3 cups sugar
5 cups flour
2 tsp. salt
5 tsp. baking soda
1 tsp. cinnamon
1 tsp. cloves
1 tsp. nutmeg
4 eggs, beaten
1 cup salad oil
1 qt. buttermilk
2 tsp. vanilla

Mix raisin bran, sugar, flour, salt, soda, and spices in large container. In another bowl, combine eggs, oil, buttermilk, and vanilla. Add liquid ingredients to dry ingredients and mix thoroughly. Cover container and put in refrigerator. When ready to use, stir thoroughly to distribute oil through the batter. Bake in greased muffin tins at 400 degrees for 15 minutes. Makes about 24 muffins. Batter will keep for six weeks.